CALIFORNIA GOES GREEN

A Roadmap to Climate Leadership

Michael R. Peevey

Diane O. Wittenberg

ISBN-13: 9781545577301
ISBN-10: 1545577307
Library of Congress Control Number: 2017906546
CreateSpace Independent Publishing Platform
North Charleston, South Carolina

CALIFORNIA GOES GREEN

A Roadmap to Climate Leadership

———

Dedicated to all Californians whose encouragement and support for progressive climate change policies and advanced energy programs have made the state a worldwide model of what a free, committed, and resolute people can do, with special recognition to governors Edmund G. (Jerry) Brown Jr. and Arnold Schwarzenegger.

———

CONTENTS

ABOUT THE AUTHORS

Michael R. Peevey has worked in California energy across all its facets: as a corporate officer in a Fortune 500 company, an entrepreneur, and president of California's most powerful energy regulatory agency, the California Public Utilities Commission (PUC), for a dozen years. He earned bachelor's and master's degrees in economics at the University of California, Berkeley, before starting his career as an economist in Washington, D.C. In 1973 he helped found the California Council of Environmental and Economic Balance (CCEEB), an organization of unions, businesses, government, and others. Peevey was the CCEEB's president until 1984, when he joined Southern California Edison Company, one of the nation's largest electric utilities, as a vice president. He became president in 1990.

In 1995, two years after leaving Edison, he co-founded New Energy Ventures, an energy supply and services company later sold to AES for $92 million. Now named New Energy, the company remains one of the largest energy supply and services companies in the country, with revenues in the billions. When the energy crisis of 2000-2001 hit California, Governor Gray Davis asked Peevey to be his chief adviser through the troubled times. In 2002 Davis appointed him to the PUC and made him president. Peevey continued in that role under Davis and governors Arnold Schwarzenegger and Jerry Brown. He retired from the PUC at the end of 2014, turning his attention to writing this insider's account of California's storied environmental and energy policies over the last forty years.

Diane O. Wittenberg has extensive experience in California environmental and energy policy. Joining Southern California Edison in 1985, she became vice president of corporate communications for both the electric utility and its holding company, Edison International (EIX). She also served as president of a non-regulated EIX subsidiary, Edison EV, which provided electric vehicle charging installations for six major automakers. After leaving Edison, Wittenberg became the founding president of the California Climate Action Registry, a nonprofit formed through state legislation. The Registry developed greenhouse gas accounting and inventory standards. Wittenberg also served as president of the organization that subsequently evolved from the California experience, The Climate Registry, which developed voluntary greenhouse gas reporting standards for forty-one states, the twelve Canadian provinces and six Mexican states.

In 2011, Wittenberg became the first executive director of the PEV Collaborative, a public-private partnership to help insure electric vehicles were a commercial success in California. Members of the collaborative include the three key environmental and energy agencies in California, the major car companies and electric utilities operating in the state, the legislature, the governor's office, and large environmental organizations. She is chair of the California State Parks and Recreation Commission.

FOREWORD
By Joseph P. Kennedy II

More than thirty years ago, I flew from Boston to Los Angeles and was met at the airport by a young utility executive who had been assigned the task of getting me in and out of a meeting with Southern California Edison Chairman, CEO and President Howard P. Allen.

Michael R. Peevey, sporting long hair and driving a convertible, cautioned on the drive into the city that my pitch for SoCal Edison to save money for ratepayers by buying cheap surplus electricity that Citizens Energy Corporation would wheel from Utah to California might not be well received.

It had been just a few years since I had launched Citizens Energy Corporation, a unique nonprofit dedicated to using revenues from successful energy ventures to assist the poor. After a promising start in the oil business, we sought to become the first non-utility to sell power across state lines and were hoping to make SoCal Edison our first customer and its ratepayers the beneficiaries of lower-cost energy.

As it turned out, Peevey was quite right. Howard Allen's office, plastered with photos of him with Richard Nixon, gave a hint of what was to come. He flatly refused to buy the power, even though we were substantially undercutting prevailing market power prices, and threw me out of the office.

Though we didn't end up getting the deal with SoCal Edison, Citizens Energy did manage to break the electric utility cartel, challenging the industry by winning a landmark Federal Energy Regulatory Commission ruling allowing us to buy and sell wholesale power across the country. Our first offer, to sell cheap electricity to save money for Los Angeles city customers, made us the first non-utility broker of electricity and helped jump-start the modern multibillion-dollar power trading industry.

And in Peevey, who encouraged me on the ride back to the airport to continue the fight, I found someone sympathetic to our mission. He fully embraced what we were trying to do—to make energy more affordable for the poor through innovative energy ventures. Even then, he was working on efforts to increase the share of renewable power in California's energy mix. He was looking far into the future.

Peevey and Wittenberg's book, *CALIFORNIA GOES GREEN: A Roadmap to Climate Leadership*, chronicles the events that created the nation's leading green energy state. From the first stirrings of California's environmental movement to reduce smog, to its current role as a global pacesetter to stem global warming, these two energy insiders cover history they not only witnessed but also helped shape. Peevey's career has traced an arc from environmental activist to utility executive to energy entrepreneur to leading regulator. The paths of Wittenberg and Peevey first crossed at Southern California Edison, where she was a vice president. She went on to play a key role in paving the way for the growth of zero-emission electric vehicles in the state as president of Edison EV, and creating landmark reporting standards for greenhouse gas emissions throughout North America.

When you look at how far California has come in its fight against global warming, you have to recognize clean energy veterans like Peevey and Wittenberg, who were present as early steps to protect the environment evolved into a movement that now spans the globe. When my father, Robert F. Kennedy, served in the US Senate, he stood up to the combined forces of the tobacco and advertising industries to place surgeon general's warnings on every packet of cigarettes. Many scoffed at that initial step, but over the last fifty years, public awareness of the dangers of smoking have heightened, cigarette advertising has disappeared from the airwaves, and smoking rates have dropped by close to two-thirds. What was once a quixotic mission has now become a broadly accepted global campaign. So it is with the fight to control climate change: Through the work of people like Peevey and Wittenberg, climate change consciousness and the fight to contain it have become mainstream values of public concern.

Since my first meeting with Peevey, Citizens Energy has evolved to start building utility-scale solar arrays, wind farms and green transmission lines with partners like San Diego Gas & Electric. One of those lines, the high-voltage Sunrise PowerLink, carries renewable energy from the remote Imperial Valley of California to San Diego. We use 100 percent of our profits to help the poor with their energy needs through measures like installing solar collectors atop the homes of low-income families in the Imperial Valley, the poorest corner of California, at no cost to the homeowners.

Our transition has closely followed, on a smaller scale, what the authors of this book describe—embracing a set of values committed to a healthy planet and creating a roadmap to achieve the changes needed to protect our environment for future generations. That model has endured through state Democratic and Republican administrations.

This book shows how strong, bipartisan leadership in the nation's most populous state and the world's sixth-largest economy led to incremental changes over five decades to move closer and closer to fully living the gospel of renewable power, energy efficiency, and clean technology, with economic payoffs in the form of business and job growth.

And it's all been accomplished in service of a profoundly moral goal—to protect our land, air, water, and oceans, along with the plants and animals that inhabit our planet, from the devastating impacts of global warming.

Who hasn't become convinced that our climate has been changing, evidenced by frequent reports of tragedy caused by freakish weather? Heat waves, rising in frequency and intensity, are becoming routine, especially hurting the poor and elderly residents who can succumb to heat-related causes when temperatures soar to over 110 degrees for extended periods. The impact of extended drought on the West Coast has dried up water supplies, endangered agriculture and sent the price of food from America's breadbasket soaring. Wildfires, burning longer and hotter and more often, have scorched millions of acres and destroyed hundreds of homes in California in recent years. And when rain finally comes, it falls with a vengeance, causing mudslides and floods and wiping out homes.

In the 1980s, as a Southern California Edison executive, Peevey pushed the utility on its commitment to renewable energy, rising to president on the strength of policies that turned away from fossil fuel generation of electricity and instead embraced a clean energy future. During his twelve-year tenure as president of the state Public Utilities Commission, the state aggressively expanded energy efficiency measures, created thousands of good-paying jobs while cutting per capita electricity use to half the national average, and increased commitments to getting electricity from renewable resources. California now draws more than 25 percent of its power from renewable resources and is well on the way to reaching a statutory goal of 50 percent by 2030, while reducing carbon emissions 40 percent below 1990 levels by 2030. The price of solar energy has fallen to the point where it's often cheaper than the average price of power paid by utilities. Millions of smart meters have been installed at homes and businesses, saving consumers energy and dollars. The electric car industry is thriving in the state due to tough emissions and low-carbon fuel standards backed by regulators, legislators, governors, academics, advocates, and business leaders. In each step of the process, Peevey has made sure that the benefits of energy efficiency and clean energy are extended to every Californian, regardless of income.

The authors have decades of firsthand experience as California policymakers and businesspeople. Their knowledge and insights, and that of dozens of other environmental and energy players interviewed for this book, are reflected in its pages, giving a fresh, first-person perspective on why and how California earned its sobriquet as a global leader in environment and energy.

In *CALIFORNIA GOES GREEN*, Peevey and Wittenberg draw on their deep experience to provide a thorough account of the state's leadership in battling global warming, including profiles of some of the leading figures in that crusade. The lessons they draw are clear: Progress on climate change must be bipartisan, engage stakeholders and the public, involve strong public agencies, and link environmental protection to public health, the economy, and jobs.

Their book can serve as a policy guide for nerds, a clean energy bible for true believers, or a manifesto for change agents of any persuasion. Most important, it clearly serves as a road map to achieve what has been accomplished in California's laboratory of climate change innovation.

INTRODUCTION

Climate change is the challenge of the twenty-first century; the need to combat it is immediate. While in some quarters that may seem a Herculean task that can't come easily or quickly, with strong leadership, any city, state, province, or nation can implement a long-term, successful climate leadership strategy. As the experience of California demonstrates, lowering carbon emissions demands political focus, intellectual acumen, new values, and a path that everyone—citizens, politicians, policy experts, academics, environmentalists, liberals, and conservatives—work on together and shape over time. The outcome of the 2016 US presidential election makes state and regional leadership increasingly important. California, the global sixth largest economy, behind the United States, China, Japan, Germany, and the United Kingdom, has demonstrated that progressive environmental and energy policies can benefit an entire nation, while a return to the past as President Trump is advocating, can have dire consequences.

The world is at a crossroads. It can choose to follow the course of President Trump, gutting progressive energy and air quality policies across the board, or its people can choose to develop a path like California's—emphasizing dynamic economic growth and a healthy population resulting from policies and programs that sharply reduce greenhouse emissions. We can all have much cleaner air while significantly reducing society's negative impacts on our Earth.

This book shows in unvarnished fashion how success is being accomplished in the Golden State. Setbacks abound, but the environment improves. *CALIFORNIA GOES GREEN* is based upon lessons learned in a state that is widely recognized as a leader in climate change action. But these lessons are not unique. They are cautionary tales of success, failure, bullheadedness, big spending, political chess, and, ultimately, a triumph in the creation of a new California energy and environmental ethos around preventing and adapting to climate change.

Californians initially didn't plan where they would end up. But retracing the California path offers a distillation of progress, insights, and missteps from which others can learn and adapt to their own situations. The California experience provides optimism for those who want to create new leadership, bring people together, and both coax and compel progress.

Transformative climate policy is built upon the key belief and simple notion that healthy citizens create economic vitality. In supporting that idea, society recognizes and accepts that the economy is strongest when underpinned by a clean environment, technology investment, and overall sustainability. This is the expansive, and sometimes expensive, point of view that Californians came to embrace, a view not found in Washington, D.C. today.

This book seeks to answer the often-asked question: why and how did California emerge as a global leader in energy policy, protection of the environment, and climate action? After all, successful, forward-looking policy is not always a California hallmark. Consider the long-term issues of water and sprawl, two landmark areas where the state has largely ignored its problems for decades. Climate action tells a better story.

The modern movement for a cleaner environment traces back to an early, intractable problem that began to be noticed shortly before the state's massive postwar population boom in the mid-twentieth century. In the early 1940s, Angelenos appropriated a word common in London—smog: a soup of smoke and fog. It was a perfect definition for the condition that persists and propels California's climate policy today.

When children were wheezing at age six and couldn't play outside because their asthma was too bad, dirty air was added to the roster of social ills. When middle-class and rich kids regularly crashed their bikes into parked cars because the air was too smoggy for them to see a safe distance ahead, air became a political problem. Asthma, bronchitis, allergies, and burning eyes hit everyone. There was no opting out. Even the very wealthy couldn't claim, "Not in my backyard!" and put up a wall against air.

L.A. SKYLINE WITH CITY HALL, 1956
COURTESY OF GETTY IMAGES

Because all Californians demanded clean air, solving air quality problems became the province of elected leaders and civil servants of every stripe, many of whom have served in several different segments of society: business, nonprofits, academics, as gadflies, and more. Heads of Fortune 500 companies previously ran big state agencies. Environmental leaders were also professors at Stanford, California Institute of Technology (Caltech), and campuses of the University of California and California State University. Scientists became entrepreneurs. Even actors became governors, twice, and a US senator, once.

This broad-based experience in problem solving is an important key to the state's path to leadership, on both the Republican and Democrat sides of the aisle. A side benefit of this bipartisanship has been a constancy of approach to environmental problems that varied little, no matter who was head of the state, a city, or an agency. Always in the picture has been a citizenry demanding a healthy environment.

Building an intricate web of environmental policies and practices did not occur swiftly, or smoothly, however. There were definitely enemies in the drama. Because California's economy is so large,[1] if "environmental leadership" was going to gore the ox of a mainline, large industry in the state, blood and dust would ensue before anything settled down. Enemies didn't always stay slain. Heavy industry covered California: power plants, cement factories, automotive plants, oil refining, and manufacturing. Some cleaned up. Some moved out. Some are still fighting.

Since World War II, California has had a largely continuous growth trajectory. It passed New York as the most populous state in 1962, and there was rejoicing in the streets of the Golden State.[2] It vies with Texas for the biggest year-to-year economic growth, and two states with more opposite views of long-term sustainability and economic success cannot be found.[3]

California has accomplished major changes in behaviors and values, without being measurably crazier or better at predicting the future than the nation at large. But the state has been blessed over the last forty years by a set of individuals in positions to make significant advances in policy and practice—and they did.

As Governor Schwarzenegger often said to staffers who doubted they could carry out a directive that seemed politically impossible: "I never thought I could press five hundred pounds either—until the four-hundredth time I tried it."

CHAPTER 1

A ROAD TO LEADERSHIP

The chairs were gilded. The chandeliers cascaded. The security was full metal jacket. As past evenings of chamber music hung in the air, California Governor Jerry Brown was welcomed into the 17ᵗʰ century Parisian *palais,* now home to the US ambassador to France. This was not the governor's personal style. Open shirt *sans* tie does not prevail as palace dress code. As the governor declined an offer of champagne passed on a silver salver, Ambassador Jane D. Hartley introduced him to fifty elite guests and an even larger number of media cameras. Governor Brown stood and launched the Subnational Global Climate Leadership Memorandum of Understanding, nicknamed "Under 2 MOU." In attendance that day, December 9, 2015, were scores of mayors, governors, premiers, and other regional signatories—officials who were publicly pledging to reduce carbon emissions by 80 percent to 95 percent of their 1990 levels by 2050. More than 100 jurisdictions, home to more than 600 million people and one quarter of the economic activity in the world, have signed on to this commitment.[4] Each jurisdiction has set specific midterm climate goals, and will accomplish them through projects best addressed locally, such as energy efficiency and zero-emission vehicles. This approach was a sea change from the UN's views nine years earlier.

The prevailing conceit underlying the 1997 United Nations Kyoto Agreement on climate change had been clear: A global problem like climate change could be addressed only by reduction commitments on the national or regional (European Union, for example) level. Actions taking place anywhere below nation level were derided as meaningless in effectively addressing a worldwide

1

problem.   Even as late as 2006, at the UN Congress of the Parties (COP) 12 in Nairobi, when then-California EPA Secretary Linda Adams attempted to offer UN negotiators success stories of the state's greenhouse gas reductions, the doors were literally shut in her face.

Yet nine years later, here was a US ambassador hosting a celebration of locally based greenhouse gas reductions during the COP 21 climate meeting in Paris. It was a clear acknowledgement that the Kyoto Agreement, built upon a top-down philosophy of emissions reductions, had failed.   In Paris, many nations presented a bottoms-up approach, relying on local programs to help them bring more to the table. This may prove to be a seminal reflection on how to turn the world to more measurable and practical ways to reduce greenhouse gas emissions.

The origin of Under 2 MOU was a partnership between California and the German state of Baden-Württemberg. Both governments committed to sharply reduce greenhouse gas emissions and to demonstrate subnational leadership and commitments to such reductions prior to the convening of the Paris Climate Summit.

The Under 2 MOU has more than 50 subnational governments signed up, with each committing to reduce their greenhouse gas emissions by 80 percent by 2050—the figure California has also committed to achieve by statute and executive order of governors Schwarzenegger and Brown. The signatories range from the two original partners to Baja California, Mexico; Los Angeles; New York City; Sardinia; Wales; Quebec; Ucayali, Peru; and Tocantins, Brazil.

**GOVERNOR BROWN AT THE US AMBASSADOR'S RESIDENCE DURING
THE UN CONFERENCE OF PARTIES (COP) IN PARIS, DECEMBER 2015**
COURTESY OF GETTY IMAGES

Under 2 MOU demonstrates that a collective impact to sharply cut greenhouse gases is essential and that subnational governments can act, usually quicker than their bigger brethren. The signatories agreed to collaborate on expanding the market for zero-emission vehicles (ZEVs); share research and technology on energy efficiency and renewables; have consistent and accurate monitoring and reporting of emissions; reduce short-lived climate pollutants such as methane and black carbon; and assess the impacts of climate change on their communities.

———

While Jerry Brown and other governors and mayors were being feted in baroque halls, a man who is much more comfortable in such surroundings, Brown's predecessor, Arnold Schwarzenegger, was across town celebrating another public-private partnership, R20 (the nonprofit Regions of Climate Change), which also addresses worldwide climate change through local actions. Schwarzenegger spoke to 500 parliamentarians in Paris as a guest of the European Union and United Nations. Cool roofs, energy efficiency upgrades to existing buildings, street lighting and other practical, local, climate-related projects have been put into practice across Africa, Mexico, Algeria, Europe, and the United States under R20 auspices.[5] Schwarzenegger started R20 as he left office in 2010, and continues his very active leadership of the group.

The State of California may seem to have little in common with the province of British Columbia, the state of Acre, Brazil; the region of Ile de France, France; Gujarat State, India; Nord Region, Burkina Faso; Cebu Province, Philippines, but all are founding members of R20. The organization, supported by the United Nations at its inception, consists of subnational governments, companies, nonprofit groups and international organizations. It includes more than 560 subnational and local governments worldwide.

Its purpose is to help subnational governments implement a host of initiatives, from starting climate-friendly projects, to sharing new technologies and programs in renewable energy and energy efficiency. The goal is to build as rapidly as possible a green economy worldwide from the bottom up and to convince national governments of the wisdom of doing so by developing successful projects, including cool roofs, improved LED street lighting, and energy efficiency toolkits for commercial buildings. Currently, R20 has solar projects underway in Burundi and Mali, a biofuel project in Indonesia, an LED lighting project in Brazil, a water filtration program in Nigeria and, closer to home, a sludge-to-energy project in Los Angeles.

Governors Schwarzenegger and Brown made California a world leader in addressing climate change. The state's current target of reducing climate emissions to 40 percent below 1990 levels by 2030 may be the most ambitious and achievable target in North America.[6] Even more impressive, the state has designed a clear path on how to reach the goal, and is already marching resolutely to achieve the reductions.

Under 2 MOU and R20—largely emanating from California under the leadership of these two governors—will spawn other initiatives on a subnational and regional basis throughout the world and reflect, yet again, the commitment of California to sponsor, promote, prod, and lead efforts worldwide to curb the growth of greenhouse gases. Further, it reflects the state's long history of not just pronouncing its wishes and goals, but acting upon them at home and abroad. In short, it demonstrates what leadership is all about.

––––––––––

Leadership has two components: a vision of the future and followers who support that vision. It is relatively simple to understand technical and scientific approaches for reducing greenhouse gases; the more difficult questions are: How do you make it happen? How do you get agreement? How do you cultivate political will? The latter is a lengthy process. Leaders who want to address climate action as a hallmark or legacy might build upon long-term approaches that can be emulated anywhere in the world.

Key to California's success has been to make climate policy a bipartisan action that cannot be easily torn asunder by any one dissenting leader or political party. State Republicans and Democrats fight polarized battles on many issues, including climate, but over the decades, leaders in both parties have agreed that California is too exposed to environmental problems to ignore their consequences. Climate change action represents the most recent example of cooperation across parties, political jurisdictions, business and government, even among individuals, acting for common good.

On the electric power front, the state has moved in forty years from having some in-state coal plants, to closing most of them, to not allowing coal power to be imported into California, to generating its power via 30 percent of renewables today, and then to setting a 50 percent renewables target for 2030.

Consider an earlier instance of air quality progress: In the 1940s, Los Angeles realized that a large portion of its smog came from burning trash. The city slowly started reducing the incineration. First, it limited commercial burning. Then, individual homeowners were restricted to limited hours when they could burn trash. Finally, in 1957, after years of incremental rulemaking, Los Angeles banned all backyard incinerators and began general trash pick-up in neighborhoods.

HIGHLAND PARK OPTIMISTS CLUB, 1955
COURTESY OF THE LOS ANGELES TIMES

Today, 60 years after the total ban in Los Angeles, there are still many places in the world that have no controls on open garbage incineration. Yet generating the political will to stop a simple hurtful action such as open incineration can be a first step to air quality leadership. California's air quality actions evolved slowly, from the backyard incinerator ban, to requiring cleaner-burning gasoline and automotive engine controls, to stimulating the purchases of the most electric cars of any US state.[7]

Energy efficiency standards have consistently been forged and enforced early. California set the first refrigerator and air conditioner energy efficiency standards in the mid-1970s. By 1990, there were federal standards. Today, California is enacting DVR, phone charger, and retro building energy efficiency standards.[8]

Over the years, the average Californian's electricity use has gone down, although summer temperatures and use of air conditioning have increased.[9] The continuing effort on efficiency standards by the California Energy Commission (CEC), coupled with a mild climate, has brought the average Californian's electricity use down to about half of that of the rest of the country.[10]

There is a trade-off, of course. Californians also pay more per kilowatt-hour than most Americans.[11] But their efficient appliances and insulated buildings use fewer kilowatt-hours than appliances and buildings elsewhere. As a consequence, residential electricity bills are nearly 25 percent lower overall than the rest of the country's and are trending further downward.[12] Yet even today, there are many places in the world that have no—or very relaxed—appliance energy efficiency standards. It is another easy starting place for climate leadership.

In California, every utility customer's bill contains a "public goods charge" that funds the Energy Commission's development of clean energy and efficiency technology. In 2012, Southern California Edison sought to kill the fee but lost in court, and California state government continues to spend about $160 million annually on energy efficiency and new energy sources.

The threads of California's ever-expanding environmental and energy laws and regulations have been woven into a tapestry that attracted the attention of the federal government, other states, and other countries that have adopted or will adopt many of these measures. The catalytic converter, now standard on every car, was first required on California cars in 1975; new nuclear power plants were banned in the state in the 1970s; almost 50 percent of the electric cars sold in the United States are driven by only 12 percent of the population—those who travel California roads; and Governor Brown announced in 2015 that half of all California energy must be renewable by 2030. These are examples of California leadership that, sooner or later, the rest of the world follows.

Climate change is a physical phenomenon, but addressing it is a societal action, best tackled by government. Clean water, clean air, and species protection all demand civil engagement. Governors Brown and Schwarzenegger come from different political parties, and each addressed climate priorities somewhat differently. What is notable is that they did not undo their predecessor's gains on the issue. Rather, they built on and amplified what came before.

Governments decide priorities of spending, infrastructure, land use, air, and water policies. Leadership needs steadiness and resolve.

Because leaders in a democracy come and go, many leaders of both parties must come forth over time with the same general environmental values. Every California governor since Edmund G. "Pat" Brown was elected in 1958 has not only moved the environmental football down the field, but suffered very few fumbles that reversed gains.

This bipartisanship has produced a much-needed stability in adopting policy that allows businesses and investors to plan and attract investments, manufacturing and other businesses to the state. Consider electric vehicles (EVs).[13] Their popularity in California is not because movie stars drive EVs or because the state is small and distances are short enough to run on one battery charge. No, EV ownership is steadily becoming mainstream in California because of a package of statewide public goals regarding EV dissemination, financial incentives available to buyers in low-income neighborhoods, charging availability monitored and led by the state, the making of gasoline a less attractive option financially, and a host of other policies that evolve from solid, consistent, bipartisan leadership underpinned by a full package of specific policies and incentives to get electric cars on the road.[14] [15]

Another important element in the success of California's environmental efforts has been to tie them to public health and jobs. Elected and appointed officials reflect the will of their constituents. This is seen in the panoply of California's environmental laws, regulations, initiatives, resolutions, and other rules that use the same basic rationales to fit the specific action: improving the economy overall, increasing jobs in part by creating new job categories, and providing a fairer and more equitable life for all citizens.

A common question asked of California officials is, "How do you get voters to support clean air and reduced greenhouse gases when it costs them money?" The answer has been to convince people that good environmental policies are in their own self-interest. This strategy has been successful, with the majority of Californians wanting a clean environment and supporting efforts to combat climate change.

_____

Improving and protecting public health has been a high priority for all California residents. A typical poster-image appeal for better environmental policies is a child suffering with asthma. The parallels with "no smoking" campaigns are clear. The American Lung Association is a leading nonprofit fighting against tobacco. Most medical practitioners support the group for its science-based approach to problems, and today the Lung Association calls for immediate action on the climate agenda. It makes similar points to tobacco issues: public health care costs are much lower when chronic diseases such as asthma and heart disease are fewer.[16]

Improving the economy, addressing income inequality, and creating more jobs are as important as promoting public health in gaining the public's support for environmental policies. Even in California, voters aren't noted for showering money on government. But citizens generally believe that environmental action is in their own economic interest. They equate public health with a strong economy and a healthy workforce.

Because one of the primary drivers for passing environmental laws is a stronger economy, it is essential to measure the benefit to the state from clean-economy jobs. Although California has a reputation for tough regulations and high taxes, it also has a highly skilled workforce, the highest-funded tech investment in the world, a good climate, and a gateway to Asia.[17] [18] The state is consistently ranked among the top three to five states every year in creating new jobs from new businesses.[19]

Part of this is due to jobs in water technology and services, electric vehicles, recycling, alternative energy, and battery manufacturing.[20] But another reason so many clean air technologies and the hundreds of thousands of jobs associated with them are in California is because the state both demands and supplies new clean technologies. If someone can build it, California will try it—and then mandate it if it works, from truck diesel traps to energy storage, from appliance standards to renewable power.

Every year, people move into and out of the state. On balance, more high-income people move in, and more low-income people move out, in large measure due to the state's high cost of living.[21] Part of what draws new residents is a strong economy underpinned by commitment and action to assure clean air and water and preservation of natural resources. Although many major companies move to California, many industries have left the state, taking good blue-collar jobs with them.[22] And even in the high-tech sector, home state companies like Apple, Tesla, Intel and others have expanded production and added jobs outside the state.[23] [24] [25] Balancing climate benefit and jobs is always dynamic.

Protecting the physical environment—air, water, mountains, desert, and coast—is vitally important to many people who support California's environmental efforts. California is much like other places across the globe where there are beautiful and threatened physical resources that people love: the Grand Canyon, the Amazon River, Lake Baikal, the Great Barrier Reef, glaciers, and so on. Attaching environmental measures to the reality of preserving beloved resources is a crucial link to the success of many environmental efforts. Over the years, Californians have passed laws protecting the state's natural resources, and they are often fierce in maintaining their stewardship.

California's environmental movement has had a keen focus over the years on building world-class environmental and energy agencies—the Air Resources Board (ARB), the California Public Utilities Commission (PUC), and the California Energy Commission (CEC). They have developed programs grounded in sound research produced by the state's great universities. Agencies promulgating tough new standards must be highly respected by the administrative branch, the legislature, the judiciary, and the voters. The public will not accept aggressive, leading edge climate regulations and laws unless they trust the data and science that backs them up. Judges hearing legal challenges will not affirm regulations and laws unless the underlying quality of the data is highly defensible.

Alongside their regional and national peers, state and local agencies perform high-quality, defensible modeling and data-collection to drive regulatory rules. This is good policy, gives the public confidence in its regulators, and has the benefit of helping insure the regulations stand when challenged in court.

Good government could not exist without a political will backed by strong public policy. Too often, a leader and citizenry willing to adopt good environmental policy end up adopting bad policy simply because their policy resources are wrong or nonexistent. The nexus of academic research linked directly to public policy is honored in California.

For example, Mark DeLucchi of the University of California, Davis is a global expert on automotive emissions and reductions. He recently completed a life cycle analysis of various transportation mitigation strategies. His cost-benefit rankings of the priority of implementing regulations for actions such as requiring low-friction engine oil, cargo handling equipment, anti-idling equipment, low global warming potential (GWP) refrigerant for mobile air conditioning systems, and similar practical measures were done for the ARB. The agency will use this research to decide the ranking, cost-benefit, and timing of new regulations to control greenhouse gases.

Conversely, a vested interest like a large company can also help shape policy through academic research. Business can present the virtues of a new technology or industrial process the company strongly endorses. On the other hand, sometimes businesses present complex studies showing why a proposed new regulation will drive them out of business.

In California, electric utilities fought putting selective catalytic reduction (SCR) technology on their smoke stacks, saying that they would go out of business or that electric prices would rise dramatically. State agencies did independent studies to assess costs, and stuck to their regulatory guns. When the technology was finally installed, it cost a third of what all the utility reports claimed would be true.

One can look at current research to learn what policies California is considering for the future. For example, the University of California and California State University campuses, Stanford, Caltech, and others in 2016 were studying topics that will become the basis for future policy direction, including evaluating the impact of preserving and building affordable housing in transit-oriented developments. Assuring affordable housing near public transit has been cited by many local planning agencies as a viable strategy to reduce vehicle-travel demand. This research will provide a first-of-its-kind analysis of the travel demand reduction benefits of co-locating affordable housing and transit. It will also look at the impact of co-locating high-income, car-owning families near public transit and evaluate which approach has the greatest travel-reduction impact.

The state is planning for the next generation of buildings to contribute significantly to its 2050 climate goal. Current academic research is looking at technical solutions to see if new structures could generate nearly zero greenhouse gases from energy, water, waste, and transportation impacts. The results of the study will be used to assess the cost, return, and time frame for new state policy in this area. Also, the tie-ins, in particular between the University of California and the National Laboratories at Berkeley, Livermore, and the Jet Propulsion Laboratory in La Cañada, are extremely valuable as the labs conduct cutting-edge research on energy, environmental and climate change issues.

———

It can take years of research and lots of practice to perfect strong regulations. Many trace California's seminal moment to 1973 and the Arab oil embargo. By then, California had more than twelve million vehicles on the road, and the polluted air often made breathing difficult. The oil embargo led to higher fuel costs and the production of smaller and more fuel-efficient vehicles attractive to consumers. The goal—and the result—would be lower emissions, particularly after the ARB mandated that by 1975, all new cars sold in California had to be equipped with catalytic converters.

The ensuing fight between automakers and state regulators over that issue was a dress rehearsal for how the forces on each side would line up for many years to come. For California, the catalytic converter was partly needed to address "engine knock," which had come about because of an earlier NO_x reduction rule.[26] Thus, the tradition of building a matrix of overlapping regulation had begun. California also began to refine its basic platform: "Data wins." The automakers, on the other hand, overplayed their hand on catalytic converters. It was a mistake from which they would suffer, and repeat in various ways, for decades.

When the ARB promulgated the requirement for catalytic converters, the automakers fought back, primarily with a pricing argument: Adding catalytic converters to vehicles sold in California would add $300 to the price tag of each new car, because a catalytic converter required platinum to work well.[27] Mandating platinum in the family Chevy or Ford was an outrage, automakers argued. They worked hard to keep costs down on new cars, and here was a completely extraneous call for new technology! They argued that if the catalytic converters were really needed, of course they would have added them to cars. But they were not necessary. Even the EPA believed California was overreaching.[28] Adding costs to consumer goods like cars was both cheeky and unnecessary, these critics claimed.

Everyone knows the outcome. Catalytic converters became standard issue on vehicles worldwide.

———

The influence of another mandate, the 1990 Zero Emission Vehicle (ZEV) rule, requiring that two percent of all new car sales in 1998 be ZEVS (electric and hydrogen-fueled cars), is still being debated.[29] Was the regulation a failure because it had to be pushed back in time and volume requirements? Or was it a success, because it really did encourage automakers to invest in EV production overall?

In 2015, with half the ZEVs in the United States being driven in California, the state is not even close to reaching a two percent sales penetration. In retrospect, the ARB mandated a car that the automakers could not deliver *en masse* and at a reasonable price by 1998. But would the electric car market be as developed as it is today if the ZEV rule had not been promulgated? Tesla might still be a concept car if it hadn't been financed across the years by carbon credits it sold to most other automakers so they could meet their California fleet emissions standards.[30]

Wall Street analysts realized that Tesla was selling emissions credits to other automakers for at least $5,000 per car, all of which dropped to its bottom line.[31] The company had to do nothing to make a credit except sell one of its own cars. It was all that free credit money, more than the financiers' belief in electric cars themselves, that drove Tesla stock up for years.

In another area, Energy Commission requirements both demanded and incentivized a sharp increase in appliance efficiency. Most recently, the pioneering declining rebates under the California Public Utilities Commission's (PUC) Solar Initiative spurred major increases in solar panel efficiency and decreases in cost.

The long-term, ever-expanding, complex web of innovative regulations, practices, and technologies stretches across a range of problems, from smog reduction to climate change. Vehicles, power plants, air conditioners, and efficient window glass in California are cleaner and often higher tech than elsewhere in the world.

For many years, the key California environmental and energy agencies have been "off-budget." That means that although the governor and legislature must approve how the agencies will spend their budgets, the money to fund those budgets doesn't come from the tax dollars collected by the state each year. This has been key to the long-term health and stability of the agencies, as it largely avoids the boom-and-bust budgeting dependent on each year's overall state tax collection. The agencies generate their own operating funds through fees on services, permits, fines, or dedicated funds, such as a percentage of license plate, gas tax, or utility user fees or other trust funds.

In general, the ARB has a budget of about $800 million annually and employs nearly 1,500 people.[32] The PUC budget is around $1.4 billion, and the agency employs more than 1,000 people,[33] while the CEC budget is close to $1 billion; the agency employs around 650 people.[34]

California's climate change efforts have benefitted from choosing leaders with varied backgrounds and experiences, not just lifelong politicians and bureaucrats. Americans generally see value in cross-fertilization of experience as a basis for top policy jobs, and Californians provide a good example of this. This societal value turns out CEOs, mayors, governors, and appointed officials who know environmental, policy, business, and financial aspects of issues from multifaceted experience. Many a Wall Street titan yearns to cap off his career and share his experience as a US Treasury secretary. Public service in California has the same cachet. The state often snares the best of the best for low-paying policy leadership positions that can build public legends.

For example, Mary Nichols, the longtime chair of the ARB, has also helmed UCLA's Institute of the Environment, taught in its law school, been on the board of a utility, and worked at several nonprofits and the federal government as practice for her long and successful tenure at the ARB. John Bryson was a co-founder of the national environmental group Natural Resources Defense Council (NRDC), chair of the State Water Resources Control Board, CEO of one of the state's largest utilities, Southern California Edison, and US secretary of commerce.

Former California Senator Darrell Steinberg is an example of someone whose previous experience proved beneficial to environmental action. In 2008, Steinberg, as state Senate president, introduced and guided into law SB 375, which requires each area of California to submit to the state its transportation and land use programs to reduce greenhouse gases. This law remains a vital piece of California's climate laws. Steinberg wrote the law based on his experience on the city council of Sacramento, where he gained an intrinsic understanding of how cities work and how important they are to making change happen on a larger scale. Under SB 375, plans revolve around major transit expansion, making biking and walking more attractive, and creating many new jobs within a short distance of transit hubs. Sacramento, where Steinberg was elected mayor in 2016, is a leader in this arena, and the city plans have the goal of accommodating a 39 percent population increase over the next years while simultaneously reducing auto traffic.

Many states and regions claim to follow this direction with alacrity, success, and an array of incentives aimed at attracting new jobs. They offer tax breaks, land donations, worker training, and other inducements very successfully. But low-tech jobs are not the same as jobs in new technology. And sometimes you have to give up old technology to encourage the new.

California has been able to take advantage of its place as the tech capital of the world and makes a compelling case for putting new technology into use in combatting climate change. As an example, for many decades there were several large auto plants throughout California, including Chrysler, Ford, GM, Studebaker, and Nash. Comets, Lancers, Barracudas, Ramblers, and Valiants were ubiquitous on California roads. The automakers liked being in the state that had their largest market in the country. But it became too difficult for the industry to meet air quality standards in their manufacturing and painting assembly. The last plant shuttered was a northern California facility in Fremont, jointly owned by General Motors and Toyota, which opened in 1984 and rolled off its last Tacoma trucks in April 2010.

Six months later, Tesla began a hand-assembly line for the S model in the same cavernous space. In June 2016, the Chinese-backed electric car company Atieva leased a large space nearby, where it plans to manufacture electric vehicles and employ 1,300 people. Tesla has been rolling off tens of thousands of Tesla S cars at the Fremont plant and has added Tesla X assembly.

A tour of the plant features an opportunity to go over to a row of Tesla front doors hanging in a long line in preparation for attachment to a chassis. Visitors can walk up and "help" put the car together by lifting a carbon-fiber door from the supply line with one finger and handing it over for assembly. No one ever lifted the door of a Tacoma with one finger.

Californians are used to their environmental leadership resulting in technically cutting-edge products and jobs. They see the links between environmental actions and benefits, expect them, and respond to them. Leadership requires risks, and a crucial one is to walk away from heavy industrial and polluting industries in favor of cleaner technologies. Such state practices keep ahead of the technology curve, so a dying industry doesn't need state life support for many years, living off previous successes. Advanced environmental practices that reflect stable, forward-looking policies are a magnet for all business sectors that want to know what the future looks like.

California's success in energy and environmental policy has been marked by setting public goals that can be measured and put into action. Environmental efforts need to be concrete, tracked, and publicized. California realizes the truth of the old advertising slogan, "Progress is our most important product." When it comes to climate change, data is queen. You can't manage what you don't measure. The state has always been ahead of much of the world in tracking its metrics, inventories, baselines, and models. They are indispensable elements of the California success story.

Serious climate measurement started in 2000, with a statute creating the nonprofit California Climate Action Registry. Several large companies had approached Congress, acknowledging that greenhouse gas reductions someday would be mandated. For various reasons, they wanted to reduce greenhouse gases before mandates, but they asked for a rigorous voluntary registry of those reductions over time so that their early action would be recognized and protected in the face of eventual legal requirements.

Few in Congress showed interest, so the companies knocked on California's door.

Democratic state Senator Byron Sher saw a confluence of interests: California could encourage early reductions by protecting them. The resulting California Registry developed rigorous standards for organizations to follow in tracking their own greenhouse gas inventories. Over the years the methodology was refined through use. In the end, the voluntary standards were largely adopted as regulatory standards by the ARB and the federal EPA. Many years were saved in calculating how to measure as a prelude to adopting regulations. Companies were prepared and knowledgeable about tracking and reducing greenhouse gases. Agencies could move directly to determining how, and how much, to reduce.

But even more important as watchdogs are all the local and national environmental organizations. They are resolute in their citizen oversight, knowledgeable about the law, and more litigious than the media would ever be. It is one of their most important functions. No longer is it quite so easy to have a law on the books and not enforce it. And, of course, government agencies often monitor themselves and report their progress on goals regularly and transparently.

It is easy for a politician to declare a long-term goal that sounds good. Voter cynicism often sets in if the elected official will be long gone when it becomes time to enforce that goal. That is not so much the case in California anymore. Governor Schwarzenegger and the legislature set ambitious greenhouse gas reduction goals in 2006, and Governor Jerry Brown continued the work his predecessor had begun. Brown announced in January 2015, the beginning of his fourth and last term, an executive order to reduce greenhouse gases even further. He believed the path to reaching these aggressive new goals was clearly charted, and the latticework of California regulation already in place would assure the goal's success.

———

Once the California legislature clearly sees the path forward, it will often codify executive-order goals into law, so they will not be undone. Many of the legal, regulatory, tax, policy, and other actions needed are put into place to assure the goals will be reached.

The three 2030 targets are very measurable, simple, and clear: to reach 50 percent renewable energy for electricity production, to cut California petroleum use by 50 percent, and to double energy efficiency in existing buildings and develop cleaner heating fuels by 2030.

Milestones to reach the goals are in place. These are definitely stretch goals, and there will be adjustments along the way. One big issue: how do you provide incentives for individual homeowners and commercial building owners to continually update their buildings' energy efficiency? California officials are not quite sure, but they will try different strategies. This third goal could be the most difficult to reach; its progress will be watched carefully to see whether and how it can be attained.

Big polluters and environmental activists are often natural enemies. Sometimes one side wins a skirmish, sometimes the other. Often there is compromise, and environmental progress is incremental but inexorable. However, another key to pursuing progress is to recognize that when compromise does not work, it is important to defang, co-opt or move out enemies—or just move on the cleaner technologies. An example of compromise not working in California involved automakers, cement plants, and power, to name three big industries.

As stated earlier, California was once home to many automakers that closed shop when their manufacturing practices could not keep up with the state's clean air regulations.

A similar, if less publicized, fate happened to cement plants, which were located in the California desert. Cement is heavy; plants usually like to locate as close to their end market as possible. California building has always been growing—often booming. Being in the desert meant that sand, one of the key components of cement, was always plentiful and nearby. But dust emissions and chromium content, which did not meet air quality requirements, pushed many of the plants from California. Manufacturers still want to be near the California market, so many plants now cluster right across the California/Nevada border.

Power production was also in the line of fire for air quality regulation. In 2000, 11 percent of California electricity was generated by coal. Today, it is seven percent. By 2026, coal will be near zero in the generation mix. This phase-out has had a major impact on Wyoming, Utah, Arizona, New Mexico, and other states that relied on exporting coal power to California. But the "No coal, even by wire" policy has prevailed.

To make up that portion of electricity production, the legislature and the PUC ruled that utilities in California had to generate 20 percent of their electricity via renewables by 2020. To the power companies, this was considered shocking, unfair, and impossible. But then, when it looked like the utilities were actually going to meet the goal, Governor Schwarzenegger's administration increased the renewables target. And Governor Brown, with the tepid support of the power sector, has announced that California power will be 50 percent renewable by 2030.

The biggest air quality and climate issue regarding the industrial sectors remaining in California is oil—oil refining and gasoline use. Refineries still exist in California, but no new ones have been built since the 1960s. This means that local air quality has slowly improved, as old refineries close or clean up. But the supply of gasoline for transportation has not been constrained by lack of refineries. Like cement and motor vehicles, the compromise is that gasoline can be refined in other places and shipped into California.

As the number of vehicles on the road increased to more than thirty million cars and trucks, the amount of pollution and greenhouse gases that spewed into the air outpaced the value of all the other clean technologies put in place throughout the state. California decreed that refiners had to mix additives into gasoline to make it cleaner. The state imposed additional gasoline taxes at the pump. All this raised prices for consumers. On any given day in 2016, gasoline costs California consumers about 54 cents a gallon more than the average pump price in the United States. This hasn't cut down driving appreciably, though Californians do often drive smaller cars.

Oil companies have not gone easily or sweetly into a clean future. One of the biggest employers in the state is Chevron. One of the most powerful lobby organizations is the Western States Petroleum Association (WSPA). One story draws the current battle lines. This chapter began with a description of Governor Jerry Brown's leadership on climate issues while at the climate summit of the UN meeting in Paris in December 2015. The previous month, in preparation for that meeting, he announced a new executive order consisting of three main goals, also referenced earlier in this chapter: *By 2030, California electricity would be 50 percent renewables, it would use 50 percent less gasoline for transportation fuel, and it would increase its energy efficiency by 100 percent in residential and commercial buildings.*

These goals were not developed with the motivation of "I've got to give a speech tomorrow; let's think of something that will make some news." Remember, California has a deep bench of world-class technocrats. Governor Brown had tasked them with coming up with realistic stretch goals that they believed the state could reach using *current legal and administrative authority.* The thousands of state employees working in the Air Resources Board, the Public Utilities Commission, the Energy Commission and other agencies lifted their eyes from spreadsheets, air-quality modeling tools, and new technology assessments.

They more deeply studied developing technologies with both expert and jaundiced eyes, commissioned studies and modeling from some of the state's research centers at UCLA, UC Berkeley, UC Davis, UC Irvine, Stanford and Caltech. They took a guess at what they thought was reasonable, and then discounted their guesses. The technocrats came up with goals they knew how to carry out and had the regulatory authority to enforce.

Then, legislators decided that they wanted to codify the executive order into law, so they introduced SB 350. There were several reasons for this, cutting across both practical and self-serving motives. The legislature often codified executive orders they liked. The lawmakers liked to be in charge, get their names on good bills, and have the credit for environmental leadership, too. Also, since a law ensured that the goal would stay in place after the governor's term ended, this was a signal to industry to take the executive order and upcoming bill seriously.

Governor Brown neither needed nor wanted this bill.

He knew that the accreted responsibilities of his key agencies that had been accumulated from various laws over the years were enough to get to attain the numbers without *any* new legislation. He would have preferred just to have his order implemented. But he also knew politics. If legislators wanted some reflected glory for passing these new measures, why not add some cement to the super glue?

Others saw the opportunity of the bill differently. An executive order is issued by the governor and has the force of law while he is in office. A bill, however, goes through a democratic process. The introduction of SB 350 became another bite at the apple for those who did not like the goals set out by the governor. Chief among them were the petroleum producers. A 50 percent reduction of gasoline fuels by 2030? Ridiculous! This was first time the group had ever taken that goal seriously. The governor's executive order could be gone after the 2018 elections. But this bill could be law forever.

The petroleum producers association is arguably the strongest lobby in the state. The big oil refiners and the small gasoline-station owners are on the same team. All the big and small oil companies are clear-eyed and experienced in knowing that California is *not* Las Vegas. It is the opposite. What starts in California does not *stay* in California. It is pushed out, tweaked, and adopted quickly by a dozen or so other states. Then the federal government creates a slightly easier standard and makes the whole country follow it. And people all over the world check in to see what they can do that is similar.

No. The oil companies knew from bitter experience that California is where you stand and fight. And this fight was sophisticated, thoughtful, and high-stakes on both sides.

The battle engaged on several fronts. For the public fight, the oil companies made and ran thousands of television ads portraying a world of gasoline rationing, mobility restrictions, and surcharges on minivans. The ads assured everyone that the biggest effects would be on low-income people in the farming valleys of the state. Most important, all of these measures would be undertaken by unelected, arrogant, unaccountable, and unresponsive bureaucrats—primarily the Air Resources Board.

Mary Nichols, the ARB chair, who is not fairly characterized by any of those descriptors other than "unelected," immediately took a long-planned vacation to Eastern Europe to avoid getting the agency ensnared in the politics. Meanwhile, the petroleum lobby, which contributes to almost all the legislators generously each year, started pulling in its chits on this vote.

Although Governor Brown originally neither wanted nor needed this bill, now, if it did not pass, it was a direct reflection on his leadership. He did not want to have to go to Paris and say, "We tried and failed to pass this bill."

Sensing this embarrassment factor, the oil industry moved in for the kill. In secret meetings the group agreed to support the 50 percent language—*if* it could also add some ancillary language about ARB. This additional language would essentially gut the agency and render it ineffective by expanding its board to insure dissention and making its members as argumentative and as polarized as Congress is these days. A 50 percent reduction in gasoline use would never happen with the board under "new ownership" that wasn't focused, united, and fully dedicated to climate change action.

It was a brilliant bait-and-switch ploy, and a less experienced governor might have gone for it. He would have had his legacy assured for the Paris climate meetings, and later could rationalize that what happened after he was out of office was out of his control.

But Jerry Brown doesn't roll that way. Instead, à la Governor Schwarzenegger when the EPA temporarily denied his request to let California toughen auto emissions standards, Brown lost his temper. He was furious at the attempted manipulation. The governor knew he didn't need the law to do what he had already announced in his executive order. So, he did not compromise to pass the law. He stood firm, and the bill failed.

Shortly thereafter, the ARB adopted a stringent Low Carbon Fuel Standard conceived by Governor Schwarzenegger's chief of staff, Susan Kennedy. The state is now on its way to a 50 percent reduction in transportation fuel by 2030.

This chapter has shown how other states and nations, and even smaller jurisdictions, can navigate California's road map to successful climate change action of their own. A final significant step is to turn to celebrities—artists, actors, athletes, and others—whose words of support can help the cause enormously. It's fairly easy in California, where about a half-million people work in the film industry Many among them are megaphones for many issues, including climate change. Think of *Avatar*, *Happy Feet*, and *The Day after Tomorrow*, a film about a catastrophic climate change disaster in which a new Ice Age kills everyone who can't reach the warmer southern climates. In real life, Leonardo DiCaprio drove up to the premiere of his movie *J. Edgar* in an electric Fisker.

True, not every place has a Hollywood. But every place has celebrities the local residents respect. New York has Broadway. Scores of cities have professional sports teams and high-profile businesspeople who might be recruited to speak out for environmentally progressive issues. Environmental groups have recognized the value of celebrity spokespeople for many years. The NRDC has worked with famous leaders over time to help them "green" their operations, educate them on environmental activism, and encourage them to personally and publicly live the values they espouse. Celebrity environmentalists are unparalleled in their ability to support policy solutions, rally followers, and convert doubters to become champions of all things green.

Leaders can use their persuasive force of character to bring every possible public face in their community to their side as spokespeople and cheerleaders for sound climate policy. Who are the top businesspeople, sports figures, arts leaders, up-and-coming politicians? When they support good policy, they should receive credit, thanks, and publicity and be relied upon to promulgate the message widely.

————

The following chapters detail how California, over the past forty years, developed new and dramatic energy and environmental policies that have culminated in its massive commitment to radically reduce its greenhouse gas emissions between now and 2050. There are detours, setbacks, and policy failures along the way. But overall, the state embarked on a new path that has met with acclaim and success. These stories provide much of the behind-the-scenes "color" as new policies and programs were initiated, adopted, and occasionally cast aside.

CHAPTER 2

A CALIFORNIA SNAPSHOT

California, with its population of nearly forty million, is beset with high housing prices, weak water policy, poverty, and a seemingly negative attitude toward businesses. But the state continues to be a beacon, with thousands of newcomers, foreign and domestic, becoming residents each month. The state had a $2.7 trillion gross domestic product in 2016; if California were a stand-alone economy, it would be equivalent to Britain or France.[35] [36] The state works well for most of its occupants; few trade it for any other locale.

The economy and population grew at a rapid clip in most years. More new businesses start up in California than in any other state each year. Almost all of the Fortune 500 top 50 companies have headquarters or large operations in the state.[37] In 2016, California added 433,400 new jobs. One of the largest populations of US military personnel is stationed in California.[38] Many immigrants who reside in California become US citizens each year. All of these constituencies are traditionally politically conservative.[39] Why have they consistently joined their more liberal brethren in supporting expensive new environmental and energy policies and technologies? Why do they like a strong government hand promoting the greater good, sometimes at the expense of protecting individual and corporate freedoms and wealth?

Every major energy and environmental advance has been fought over, often bitterly. Various business interests and government agencies opposed the most expensive new policies in every way they could. But citizens vote the other way. An example is the 2010 ballot initiative to gut California's landmark 2006 global greenhouse gas emissions reduction statute, the most advanced global warming legislation in the world. It was passed by a Democratic-majority legislature and signed by Republican governor Arnold Schwarzenegger.

The ballot initiative to repeal the law four years after it passed was overwhelmingly rebuffed, even at a height of the recession.

Jobs were being lost, homes were being foreclosed, and the state was teetering under a $27 billion deficit.[40] In the face of great financial woe, voters decided (62 percent to 38 percent) to keep the tough environmental law.

How California climbed to the apex of policy leadership is complex. Dirty air drove much of the effort. So did love of the state's coast, mountains, and fragile deserts. And Californians are young, compared with the average age of the population in other states.[41] They see themselves as glam and fashion-forward. They believe they can have it all—a clean environment and a strong economy. They also support hard-fighting, sophisticated environmental and social justice movements.

Citizens chose enough outstanding mayors, governors, and regulators over the years to build and retain leadership. Strong local, regional, and state agencies were noted not for slow-moving bureaucracies and indifference, but respected for in-depth technical expertise. As stated earlier, there are three powerful, large energy and environment state agencies: the California Public Utilities Commission (PUC), the California Air Resources Board (ARB), and the California Energy Commission (CEC). California has world-class universities: the ten University of California campuses, California Institute of Technology (Caltech), Stanford, the University of Southern California, the twenty-three campuses of California State University, and the California-based National Laboratories win Nobel prizes and produce thousands of dissertations on environment and energy topics.[42]

Because the leadership has been both political and intellectual, it can move mountains. Venture capitalists and software and clean tech entrepreneurs are famous for walking out the doors of Stanford and setting up shop just a few blocks from where they graduated.[43] San Jose State University, twenty miles away, staffs those businesses by graduating a thousand engineers each year.[44] Many Silicon Valley companies build products to fulfill unknown and unmet needs, and regulations that are not even on the books yet. California regulators are well known for their openness to new clean technologies. The agencies pilot and test new equipment and are not slow to require technology that improves the environment, if it passes a long-term cost-benefit analysis. There is a straight line in California from energy-efficient light bulbs to the Tesla, in that both, along with many other products, resulted from the virtuous circle of policies stimulating new technology investments or vice versa.

The environmental movement honed its own political skills in the state. Activists learned when a grass-roots campaign was effective, when a mass appeal to public health worked best, and when just suing every agency around was the strategy to pursue. Hollywood also got into the act. It provided both an educational tool and a grass-roots elixir upon which the environmental community could capitalize.

Environmentalists spend a lot of time educating screenwriters and taking them on field trips around issues that are then reflected in screenplays. Think of *Avatar, Frozen, Happy Feet*, and *Erin Brockovich* as a broad base of examples. Actors and producers including Robert Redford, James Cameron, and Leonardo DiCaprio walk the walk and are role models of political integrity. Hollywood has always provided depth, cachet and the ability to communicate with the public to support environmental values.

These examples illustrate the threads that by now have become a dense tapestry of ever-expanding environmental and energy laws and regulations, many of which later are adopted by the federal government, other states or other countries. Why was the catalytic converter, now standard on every car, first required on California cars forty years ago? What is important about the fact that new nuclear power plants were banned in the state in the 1970s? Why are 50 percent of the electric cars sold in the US driven by only 12 percent of the population, Californians? And who cares that Governor Brown announced in 2015 that half of all California energy must be renewable by 2030? These are all examples of California leadership that, sooner or later, the rest of the world follows.

One reason for progress was a similarity of policy thrust on environment and energy, no matter which political party was in power. Over the past 50 years, Democratic Governor Edmund G. "Pat" Brown lost to Republican Ronald Reagan, who was succeeded by Democrat Jerry Brown, who was followed by Republican governors George Deukmejian and Pete Wilson. Democratic Governor Gray Davis came next and was followed by Republican Arnold Schwarzenegger, who was elected when Davis was recalled by the voters in 2003 because of the California energy crisis caused by energy deregulation. Elected next was a Democrat - a recycled Jerry Brown, who returned in 2010 and then was reelected to an unprecedented fourth term in 2014. The legislature likewise shifted briefly from Democrat-controlled to Republican-controlled and then back again.

Through all that time, to use a football analogy, energy and environmental politics was played within the forty-yard lines, and California teams had a big defensive line supporting the offense: the Public Utilities Commission, Air Resources Board, and the Energy Commission. The granddaddy is the PUC. Many would carry the analogy further and say the agency is the most irascible, too. Formed by an initiative amendment to the California Constitution in 1911, the PUC was set up in San Francisco, a comfortable ninety miles away from the state capital, Sacramento. The idea was to protect these regulators from lobbying. An unintended consequence was that the agency was also far from the pesky oversight of governors and legislators.

Originally the Railroad Commission, the PUC was created to regulate the powerful Southern Pacific and lesser railroads and to monitor transportation prices they charged. Later, its power was expanded to gas, electric, and water utilities, telecommunications and passenger-transportation companies, including airlines; its name was changed to the California Public Utilities Commission in 1946. Always considered too independent by its Sacramento peers, this suspicion is compounded by the reality that the agency is periodically accused of pandering to those it is supposed to regulate and not being responsive to its own political leadership, as numerous governors have experienced.[45]

The PUC has far-reaching powers, though occasionally its wings are clipped, such as when the legislature created the California Energy Commission in 1974, in effect transferring some of the PUC's responsibilities to it. In 2016, the legislature again addressed the power of the PUC, insisting on more public transparency of its records and meetings.

A serious falling out occurred between Governor Gray Davis and his PUC president, Loretta Lynch, when California's energy crisis from 2000 to 2002 was in full disaster mode. The president of the commission needed to step in and calm the waters. Lynch did not agree with the governor on strategy to deal with the crisis, and a stalemate ensued. Davis demoted Lynch and appointed former utility executive Michael Peevey (co-author of this book), a PUC board member, to replace Lynch. Before the crisis was all over, Californians ended up paying $42 billion more in electricity prices[46] due to energy supply manipulation and price gouging, led by Enron.

The PUC, often controversial and frequently in the news, has tried to be cutting edge, a proponent of direct and lasting change in the energy-environmental arena. Nationally, it is the pacesetter,[47] and its presence is felt far beyond the borders of California.

Today the PUC remains headquartered in San Francisco, with offices in Los Angeles and Sacramento. Its more than one thousand employees include administrative law judges, lawyers, engineers, auditors, environmental and economic analysts, and support staff. The agency is sometimes a policy initiator and implementer. On climate change, the commission has worked closely with its sister agency, the Air Resources Board, on developing effective complementary policies to reduce greenhouse gas emissions.

In 2006, the agencies together worked on air emission standards that effectively reduced and ultimately will end the state's use of out-of-state coal. Likewise, the PUC developed the California Solar Initiative in 2007. It also has built cutting-edge policies in other arenas, most notably in telecommunications, where it essentially deregulated most of the industry (successfully this time), and in transportation, where it was the first government agency nationwide to set standards and regulations, albeit lightly, for transportation companies such as Uber and Lyft.[48][49]

Governor Pat Brown signed the law creating the California Air Resources Board (ARB), which soon became a world-class air-quality regulator. Brown's successor, Ronald Reagan, made the first ARB appointments, setting the agency on the path to global excellence. Republican Governor George Deukmejian's ARB fostered and promoted zero-emission vehicles. Governor Schwarzenegger proposed a "Million Solar Roofs," the most dramatic commitment to a distributed energy future yet seen in any state in the nation. Both Schwarzenegger's and the third and fourth Brown terms entwined energy and environment even more tightly by their strong commitment to addressing climate change. Backing up those leaders were a series of clever and fearless players who made things happen— sometimes more things than their governors sought.

And that leads back to Californians themselves. The citizens of the Golden State continue to elect the people, pass the bond issues, and support the laws and the initiatives that live up to the iconic description of "California Dreamin'." Few of the major changes of these many years could have taken place without the support or acceptance of a majority of the populace. Citizens repeatedly voiced their support for alternative-fueled vehicles, tough programs to combat smog, multiple efforts to improve the efficiency of homes and buildings, and strong commitments to reducing greenhouse gases. Voters showed their willingness to limit industrial and commercial projects that would have a negative environmental and energy impact.[50] [51]

California Democratic Senators Dianne Feinstein and Barbara Boxer, along with longtime former Democratic Assembly Speaker and San Francisco Mayor Willie L. Brown Jr., presided over decades of the environmental achievements chronicled in this book. Some of the other hundreds of people who collectively provided the environmental leadership for which California is known worldwide are profiled later in these pages. Many of them share a vision, convictions, a solid understanding of issues, positions of power, and political savvy. What one did was not undone by who came next but, more often, expanded.

Taking a longer view, the transition to more environmentally friendly policies did not come overnight; events between the end of World War II and 1975 set the stage.

For many years after World War II, California, like the nation, was consumed with growth. Pat Brown was elected governor in 1958 and proceeded to build the state's massive water system to move water north to south. New freeways were built across the state, along with new subdivisions, universities, and state colleges. The belief was in growth for growth's sake.

But unease emerged. The rapid expansion of Los Angeles and environs, new manufacturing plants, oil refineries, power plants, urban sprawl, and millions of new cars and trucks caused health-impacting smog. Few were untouched by it. Poor air quality spread throughout the Los Angeles Basin, east to San Bernardino and Riverside counties and south to Orange County. It didn't matter whether you were rich or poor, your eyes burned. No one could quite figure out why. Finally, a Caltech chemist, Dr. Arie J. Haagen-Smit, sucked millions of tons of air through giant fans into his lab and analyzed it.[52] Suddenly, Californians learned that smog was largely caused by auto tailpipe emissions.[53] In short order, Haagen-Smit was hauled out of his lab and appointed to be the first head of the California Air Resources Board (ARB).

As environmental awareness grew, so did an environmental movement, spurred first by air quality concerns but soon by concerns over ever more extensive sprawl, loss of farmland, and the cutting of beloved redwoods. In both Northern and Southern California, the environment became a political and economic issue.

Statewide, by the late 1960s, environmental concerns became mainstream, popular causes. The Wild and Scenic River Protection Act was signed by Governor Reagan, who once said of California's redwoods, "A tree is a tree, how many more do you need to look at?" (This has been widely misquoted as: "If you've seen one redwood, you've seen them all.")[54]   Many Californians feared that its more than one thousand miles of coastline would be ruined by new nuclear power plants and high-rise housing developments such as Coronado Shores in San Diego County. At one point, many new freeways pouring out to beaches were on the drawing boards.

This led to voter passage of the California Coastal Initiative in 1972, establishing the Coastal Commission to protect California's coastline. From the day it was created, the Coastal Commission has made thousands furious with its imperious behavior, but it has also protected access to the coastline and beaches for all Californians and permanently restricted coastal development.[55] Two years later, Governor Reagan signed into law the statute creating the California Energy Commission (CEC), another agency, like the ARB, destined to become a large, powerful, independent bureaucracy. California was set on a path that seldom wavered thereafter.

Reagan presided over California's early environmental efforts, setting the table for California's energy leadership by Governor Jerry Brown in the 1970s. In 1973, in response to the nation's first energy crisis caused by the Arab oil embargo, President Richard Nixon laid out a path to US energy independence, calling for 1,000 nuclear plants by 2000.[56] It was a bandwagon moment of patriotic fervor, except in California. The state instead passed a moratorium on new nuclear plants.

California started down the path to renewable energy sources with vigor. William Gould, the CEO of Southern California Edison, the electric utility serving ten million people, was an unlikely candidate to see the future in renewables. He rose through the company ranks as an engineer and was conservative by nature. But the technologist in him looked at the air quality in California; the businessman in him looked to the desires of his millions of customers.

Gould knew he could not build new coal plants; he didn't even want to. Instead, in 1979, he vowed that SoCal Edison would build *only* new renewable energy sources. He set the pace by helping develop the Pacific DC Intertie, giant transmission lines to carry hydropower from the Cascade Range in the Pacific Northwest to California. Henceforth, a big chunk of California's electric power would come from renewable water.

Before long, Gould would come to exhort his employees to research and pilot other projects in wind, solar, geothermal, and fuel cell technologies. Southern California Edison soon contracted to build, with Luz International, the world's largest solar-powered electricity generating plants, thousands of parabolic troughs in the desert that could power a small city.

The example of Luz and its successor, BrightSource Energy, are worth a close look, as they highlight the prospects and perils of new technologies, the role of government policy and process, and the ability to start anew.

BrightSource, headquartered in Oakland, was the successor company of Luz International, incorporated in California in 1979. It was founded by Arnold J. Goldman, an American who had developed his first solar energy project after relocating to Israel. The company, using parabolic trough technology, sought to build solar generating plants. Weakly capitalized, Luz was perhaps the earliest example of a major challenge for renewables—capital intensive technologies that need a number of years and significant cash infusions to get through the "valley of death" to prove their technologies and lower their costs in a market that is limited in scope and delayed by long processes. Luz struggled to find a market until SoCal Edison, under Gould's leadership, agreed to work together.

Over the 1980s, Luz built, and SoCal Edison contracted to take, 350 megawatts of solar energy from nine plants built in the Mojave Desert. The economics of these facilities was partially based on federal and state tax credits and an exemption from California property taxes. However, the tax exemption ended in 1991. This, along with the drop in oil and natural gas prices, doomed Luz. The company was unable to finance the last of its 80-megawatt projects, and it declared bankruptcy in 1991.

Goldman and Patrick Francois, a Frenchman by birth but now a citizen of Israel, formed Luz II, which relied on a new solar thermal power tower technology. In 2006, a group of founding members, consisting mainly of previous employees, formed the seeds of the new venture, located it in Oakland, and renamed the new company BrightSource Energy. Within a short period, BrightSource was able to contract for 2,600 megawatts of power to be sold to California utilities and also construct a power tower demonstration plant in Israel's Negev Desert.

The company's biggest project to date has been the construction of the Ivanpah Solar Power Facility. It started production in 2014, and at this writing remains the largest solar project in the world, 392 megawatts of solar towers in the California desert that power several hundred thousand homes. The plant covers thousands of acres of land and beams its concentrated mirrors on three power towers. Building it took less time than the regulatory state and federal permitting of the project.

The total cost of the project exceeded $2 billion, and it benefitted from a sizeable US Department of Energy loan guarantee. Without California's regulatory and legislative policies encouraging renewable energy, and the Obama administration's efforts to extend both investment tax credits and loan guarantees, no large, capital-intensive renewable energy power plant could have been completed.

Today, the high cost of construction, the large amount of capital needed, uncertainty about ongoing unit performance, the slowness and uncertainty of federal and state government approvals and permitting, and doubt about the continuation of the federal tax credit and California property tax exemption have dried up the appetite for projects like Ivanpah.

The cost and delays in construction of adequate transmission and opposition from some environmental groups, Native Americans, and others also contributed to doubts about building more large central-station solar generating plants, despite their lower per-unit costs and ability to reach larger markets. The upshot has been that BrightSource, in September 2014, announced it would not pursue other California projects and instead would focus on developing projects overseas. Shortly thereafter it announced a joint venture with a Chinese company to build large solar plants in Asia.

So, as always, the future is uncertain for pioneering companies. Certainly in California, the sharp increase in and popularity of rooftop solar has dimmed interest in central-station solar generation, with its permitting and financing difficulties. The appeal of distributed solar power is not only because it is easy to permit, but also because people like to have solar generation on their own rooftops.

However, climate change, the great challenge of our time, will require not only rooftop solar, but wind and solar renewable energy power plants, an extensive and reliable grid able to reach broad markets, a much more predictable, streamlined permitting process, and a financing structure that enables technology pioneers to survive the "valley of death."

The transition from Luz to BrightSource shows that entrepreneurs can have more than one life. Clearly, Luz-BrightSource believed in California's energy and environmental policies, and succeeded, at least for a while, to operate within them. But sustaining private sector ventures over the long haul is another matter and is beyond the state's ability alone. To meet the global warming challenge, a national policy is needed that provides a market for clean technology, a transmission highway to send clean electrons wherever they are needed, faster permitting, and assured financing.

Throughout the pioneering efforts in early solar, much of the research and development money for renewables bet on fuel cells as the likely winner.[57] Few envisioned that by 2016, those predictions would all be wrong. Fuel cells are still unrealized as major power generators. Central-station solar did not grow as envisioned. Instead, California has been inundated in the last decade with rooftop solar, largely in the residential sector. Approximately five percent of the state's electric energy today is provided by solar power.[58] The PUC, the California Independent System Operator (the state's predominant grid operator), and electric utilities are now addressing previously unforeseen issues of transmission access and overload because of "too much solar."

CHAPTER 3

THE EARLY YEARS

The California path and how it came to diverge from much of the nation took time to develop, and a few signal events helped it come to pass. Of course, there was the near-universal concern about air quality and the worsening pollution in Southern California in particular. But there were other major threats. A massive ocean oil spill made people conscious of the fragility of the coast. And there has always been fear up and down the state that the entire coastline would be overdeveloped. Both Democrats and Republicans in office began to articulate an environmental awareness.

California, like most states, was consumed with economic growth in the years after World War II. This was particularly true in Southern California, where the postwar years saw Los Angeles supplant San Francisco as the economic center and driver of the state.[59] New industries developed quickly, augmenting the dominant entertainment and aircraft industries. Manufacturing stood out, with new automobile assembly plants, rubber factories, steel mills, and a host of other endeavors.[60]

There was a huge postwar population boom, as military veterans who had been stationed in the state during the war made it their permanent home, drawn by the weather, the state's beauty, and plentiful new jobs. With all this new growth came vast housing tracts and low-density suburban sprawl. People became dependent upon private transportation—the automobile—to get around, as Los Angeles' old interurban streetcar and light rail system withered and died, due in part to the complicity of auto, rubber (tire) and oil interests.[61] But growth came at an incredible environmental cost—smog.[62] This coincided with the emerging national environmental ethic symbolized by the 1962 publication of Rachel Carson's book, *Silent Spring*. The subsequent banning of the pesticide DDT reflected a rising concern about the ill effects and unintended consequences of unbridled growth.

Governor Pat Brown had presided over much of the state's economic progress, serving from 1959 through 1966. It seemed everything got bigger: a massive water plan, new freeways and bridges, a greatly expanded higher education system, and scores of housing developments where orange groves once stood.

Brown had a Northern California point of view that wasn't really sensitive to the geology of the Los Angeles Basin, which is surrounded by mountains. Whole counties are entrapment zones where pollution from cars, trucks, power plants, and other fixed sources typically exceed health standards. Polluted air especially afflicts seniors, children, and people with heart and lung conditions such as emphysema, bronchitis, and asthma. President Obama brought national attention to the smog problem in Los Angeles when he noted in a speech that as an Occidental College student in 1979, "when I went running, the first week I was there, after about five minutes I'd start feeling a burning in my chest. And it was just me sucking in soot and smog."[63]

Smog was first noted in a big way in Los Angeles in July 1943. It was so severe that one writer noted, "Los Angeles residents believe the Japanese are attacking them with chemical warfare."[64] By 1947, forced by an ever-increasing level of smog, Los Angeles County created an air pollution control district, the first in the United States.

This was a milestone. Today, of course, there are air quality regulatory and management districts throughout the state and nation. The South Coast Air Quality Management District has adopted some of the strictest air quality standards anywhere, as has the San Francisco Bay Area Air Quality Management District.

By the mid-1950s, it was commonly accepted by scientists that cars and trucks were a primary cause of Southern California's worsening air quality. This affected everyone, rich and poor. On "bad days," the number of which increased each year, parents kept their children out of school, emergency rooms overflowed, athletic events were canceled, and visibility was near zero.[65] First-time visitors to Los Angeles could not believe how polluted the region was—comparable today with the pollution in Beijing or New Delhi. For many people, it literally hurt to breathe. And most everyone, regardless of political persuasion, demanded that government act.

It did.

California passed clean air legislation in 1967 and established the California Air Resources Board. At the federal level, Congress enacted the first Clean Air Act in 1970. Because the California law was already in place, and in recognition of the severe air problems the state faced, the federal Clean Air Act allowed one state, California, to enact stricter regulations than federal standards.[66] Still, in 1970s Los Angeles, unhealthy air was recorded more than 200 days a year, and environmental progress was not constant.[67] Dr. Arie Haagen-Smit, the first ARB chair, was ultimately fired by Governor Reagan because he attacked the smog problem too fast and furiously for the governor's taste.[68] Four years later, Haagen-Smit died of lung cancer.

California's struggle to reduce air pollution was not restricted to Southern California. There was bad air in the San Francisco Bay Area, the San Joaquin Valley, and elsewhere. But it was worse in Southern California, and it affected all people, regardless of location or station in life. This aroused an environmental consciousness that grew and grew. The fight against smog, which pitted citizens and their representatives against the automobile industry, utilities, and a host of manufacturers, helped to build the state's solid and enduring environmental consciousness, as people came to understand that economic growth and development can severely affect public health.

There were other assaults on the California landscape, most notably in Santa Barbara. On January 28, 1969, on Union Oil Company's Platform A in the Dos Cuadras Offshore Oil Field, a spill began. At the time it was the largest oil spill in United States history, at a rate of 1,000 gallons an hour for a month polluting the Santa Barbara Channel and the adjoining beaches. The spill continued at a reduced level until April 1969, blackening the shoreline from Pismo Beach, north of Santa Barbara, to the Mexican border below San Diego.[69]

The spill had an overwhelming impact upon marine life, killing more than 3,600 seabirds, dolphins, seals, and sea lions.[70] The public response across the entire state was rage. The corporate response was hapless, with Union Oil Co. (now known as Union 76) President Fred Hartley saying, "I don't like to call it a disaster because there has been no loss of human life. I am amazed at the publicity for the loss of a few birds."[71] (Hartley unsuccessfully sued *Los Angeles Times* editorial cartoonist Paul Conrad and the newspaper for referring to him as "Fred Heartless" in cartoons.)[72]

That spill, now downgraded to the third largest in the nation's history, after the Exxon Valdez spill in 1989 and the 2010 BP Deepwater Horizon spill in the Gulf of Mexico, had a lasting impact on the environmental consciousness of the nation, but particularly in California, and it was a prime factor in the growth of the modern environmental movement nationwide.[73]

The Santa Barbara spill also helped to galvanize public concern about preservation of the California coastline from development. Concern about the lack of public access to the coast was spurred north and south by a series of new oceanside communities. In Northern California, building of a planned community on the Sonoma County coast called The Sea Ranch created a strong backlash when it became clear the developer had no intention of allowing public access to the beaches and coastal trails along the ten miles of the development, even though the state Constitution gives the public ownership of the land up to the mean high tide line.[74] Then there was the prospect of building a chain of nuclear power plants along the coast, highlighted by Pacific Gas and Electric Company's ill-fated attempt to build one atop an earthquake fault at Bodega Bay, also in Sonoma County.[75]

Californians from all walks of life and all political persuasions said "Enough!" They banded together to qualify the Coastal Initiative of 1972 for the statewide ballot.[76] This effort only came after the environmental community and its legislative champions, led by Democratic State Assembly members John Dunlap of Napa County and Alan Sieroty of Los Angeles, tried for three years to enact a statewide coastal protection bill. Their failed effort was vigorously opposed by the oil companies, utilities, realtors, the County Supervisors Association and the League of California Cities, among others.

Frustrated by the legislature's unwillingness to act, voters turned to the California citizen tool of choice: the initiative process. Citizens qualified the Coastal Initiative as Proposition 20 for the ballot. It passed with 55 percent of the vote, shocking the entrenched interests. The Coastal Initiative eventually created the California Coastal Commission as a permanent part of state government.

The Coastal Commission has authority to control development along the 1,100 miles of California coast from offshore to a mile inland. The commission ensures that citizens have access to the beach all along the coast of California, whether that shore is state parkland or in front of a private mansion. Even along the beach of the two California coastal nuclear plants, there is surfing, sailing, and beachcombing. Not a single new state lease for offshore oil drilling has been granted since 1969 (although some new federal wells have been drilled).[77] Most of the California coast has remained public beaches. Even compared with many other substantial and tough California state regulatory agencies, the Coastal Commission wins as "most formidable."

To underscore the long tradition of bipartisanship, it's worth noting that the strong start of the Air Resources Board and the formation of the Coastal Commission took place under Ronald Reagan. Another landmark energy-environmental step taken by the state during his tenure was legislative passage of the California Environmental Quality Act (CEQA) of 1970, which makes environmental protection a mandatory part of every local and state agency's decision-making process. The importance of CEQA cannot be minimized. Its requirement that environmental concerns surrounding any new development must be studied and, if found to harm the environment, be mitigated or eliminated, has made such awareness a part of life for public and private decision-makers.[78] Not without controversy, and on occasion suspended temporarily by the legislature, CEQA is part of the bedrock for California decisions that affect the energy sector and the environment. CEQA is second to none as a tool to protect the natural resources of the state.

When most people think of Reagan and the environment in one sentence, they remember the infamous utterance attributed to him about the redwoods. And it is true that he once asked where the Eel River was, when he was standing next to it. Still, a dispassionate view of Reagan would see him as a transitional figure, from the go-go years of his predecessor, Pat Brown, to the "small is beautiful" and "era of limits" approach to issues of Brown's son, Jerry.[79]

A fair appraisal would note also that Reagan established the Tahoe Regional Planning Agency to address the long-term environmental challenges facing Lake Tahoe, including the loss of water clarity and the threat of overdevelopment. Equally noteworthy, working with pro-environment Republican and Democratic legislators, he blocked construction of two large dams—one on the Eel River, the other on the Feather River. [80] And, as governor, he set aside 145,000 acres of land for the state park system.[81] As Reagan biographer Lou Cannon wrote, "… no other modern California governor has come close" to this number. Further, Cannon noted, Reagan worked to acquire redwood forests, which laid the groundwork for the Redwood National and State Parks. Cannon wrote, "Several of the taller old-growth redwoods that are now stellar attractions in the national park would probably have become desks or picnic tables long before 1978 had they not been saved in the Reagan years."[82]

Certainly, his eight years as governor coincided with the fast growth of the environmental movement in California and the increased environmental tilt of the average resident.[83] Whether Reagan contributed to this growth in some instances or simply went along with the popular will is unclear. But no doubt his administration helped usher in the transition to the Jerry Brown years and kept alive bipartisanship on some major environmental and energy issues.

CHAPTER 4

EFFICIENCY, RENEWABLES, AND AIR

The Reagan era was one of transition, as environmental concerns and issues became more prominent throughout California. In response, elected representatives, government officials, and bureaucrats at all levels sought to enact and adapt to changing circumstances, especially throughout the 1970s. It was a time of new energy and environmental approaches, radical changes in attitude, great successes and abject failures.

In 1974, President Nixon resigned and flew home to his native state four months before Ronald Reagan's second term as governor ended. The previous year, the state and nation had felt the harsh impacts of the Arab oil embargo, with gasoline shortages, service station closures, the odd-even gasoline rationing system, and rapidly escalating prices.

Fall 1974 saw the gubernatorial election of 36-year-old Jerry Brown, son of former Governor Pat Brown. The elder Brown's legacy was as master builder of infrastructure.[84] His son had a "small is beautiful" philosophy. An early incarnation of that was a state focus on conserving electricity and using renewable power.[85] A powerful boost to those policies was California's turn against the national pronuclear sentiments.[86] In 1976, two years after Nixon called for 1,000 new nuclear plants, California voters defeated Proposition 15, which would have banned nuclear plants, but, when coupled with new legislation, effectively declared a moratorium on new nuclear plants. Only one nuclear plant—Diablo Canyon Power Plant—is still operating in California. However, Pacific Gas and Electric Company announced in June 2016 that it would close the plant by 2026 to develop cleaner technologies like wind and solar, aiming at the state's goal of more than 50 percent of electricity generation to come from renewable sources by 2030.[87]

The environmental community was learning how to flex its muscles in the 1970s, led by the efforts of the Natural Resources Defense Council (NRDC), the Environmental Defense Fund (EDF), and the American Lung Association, among other groups. Ralph Cavanagh of the NRDC and John Zierold, legislative advocate for the Sierra Club, championed a new state approach on energy policy, insisting on expansion of the role of energy efficiency in energy planning and a significant increase in the role of renewable resources, such as geothermal energy, wind, and solar. Along with others, Cavanagh organized environmental activists, became a fixture at the PUC and ARB, wrote many articles, and cultivated reporters, generally charming a change in energy policy nearly single-handedly.[88]

––––––––

A major California response to the Arab oil embargo of 1973 was for the legislature to pass a bill creating the five-member California Energy Commission (CEC). At the behest of the utilities and the business community generally, as well as many local governments, Reagan in 1973 vetoed the bill. But a year later, ending his last term as governor and planning to run for president in 1976, Reagan felt the need to demonstrate leadership on energy issues. So back came the bill to create the California Energy Commission, the Warren-Alquist Act.

After much fighting, the new bill squeezed through the legislature by a one-vote margin in each house. This time, Reagan signed it, leaving to his successor, Jerry Brown, the job of making the first appointments to the governing board. Looking back, one has to wonder why the utilities, which had much sway with Reagan and his staff, did not grasp a year earlier that they would have been better off if Reagan, not Brown, had chosen the CEC commissioners.

The formation of the energy commission, the third of the big three energy and environmental agencies, meaningfully altered the electrical energy industry in California. Richard Maullin, a Brown confidante, was the commission's first chairman. Maullin had clear marching orders, and he wanted both to meet and exceed the governor's expectations. The commission's other initial members were former state Assembly Speaker Bob Moretti; PUC General Counsel Richard Gravelle; renewable energy proponent Ronald Doctor, and Alan Pasternak of the Lawrence Berkeley National Laboratory.

The CEC had multiple tasks to perform, each representing a major shift in authority and responsibility from the utilities to state government. Like the ARB, the CEC was located in Sacramento, allowing the state government to keep a close eye on the new agency. Oversight of the PUC, located ninety miles away in San Francisco, continued to be difficult.

The CEC was the new kid on the block and had some big responsibilities. First, it was supposed to be a one-stop power plant siting agency. Previously, every utility made its own decisions regarding when to build a new power plant, where to build it, and how it would be powered. The utility would negotiate with the necessary local governments, seek a permit from the PUC, and a power plant would be built. The CEC formation shifted the ultimate decision-making from the utilities to state government. No longer could a utility, practically alone, decide where to site a new power plant or when to do so. This was a big change.

Next, the CEC was the lead agency for long-term energy planning. It was authorized to forecast electricity demand and supply. This was another major transfer of responsibility from utilities to government and reflected the desire of environmentalists and others to have a more objective look at the future energy needs of the state. This ended the era of utility planners who seemingly operated, in part, by holding out a thumb at arm's length, squinting, and then pronouncing, "Yep, it'll be a 5 percent growth in electricity demand next year."

Third, the CEC became the state's lead agency for the promotion of energy efficiency (called "conservation" at the time) and alternative and renewable energy research, development, and demonstration. Also, the CEC was asked to look at what is often called demand-side management and decide what it could do to reduce the growth in electricity demand through efforts like enhanced appliance standards for refrigerators and other products.

This third duty ultimately became the CEC's most important and influential raison d'etre. Since 2002, the CEC has implemented California appliance efficiency standards for hundreds of products, such as light bulbs, air conditioners, stoves, refrigerators, dishwashers, televisions, computers, public stoplights, and EV charging. Given its constituency, it has also set standards for pool heaters and wine chillers. Other states and the federal government have adopted many of the standards.

By the mid-1970s, California, by popular initiative vote, had said no more coastal power plants of any kind, and the legislature, by statute, had decreed no more nuclear power plants anywhere in the state. Policy actions forbade new coal plants.[89] The state was turning away from simply accepting the need to build new power plants hither and yon and was looking for a cleaner, more environmentally sensitive path. It found it, in part, with the legislative passage of the Private Power Producers Act of 1976.

The act encouraged the development of "non-conventional" power sources, principally renewable energy. Excluded were the more common, capital-intensive power facilities, such as nuclear, large hydroelectric projects (those over 30 megawatts) and coal.[90] Further, the statute provided for the connection of private power facilities to the utility-run electric transmission system, or grid. It also provided for the intrastate transmission of electricity from the point of generation to the points of delivery. This legislation was transformative. It opened the generation of electricity to companies other than utilities and simultaneously stimulated the development of renewable energy.

———————

Two years later, in 1978, Congress, at the urging of President Jimmy Carter, enacted the Public Utilities Regulatory Policies Act (PURPA), which emulated California law. Its goal was to stimulate small power producers of renewable energy and cogeneration. A small independent power producer was defined as a facility under 80 megawatts that produced wind, solar, biomass, or geothermal energy. Projects meeting these definitions were considered "Qualifying Facilities." Utilities were required to purchase their output at their "avoided costs" (what it would have cost for the utility to generate the power itself), to sell the new facilities' supplemental or backup power, and to interconnect them to the grid.[91]

In 2002, the CEC seized on all the renewable possibilities and set a goal of a "Renewable Portfolio Standard" of 20 percent in California by 2017. This was a clear directive, and the public and private sectors went to work to make it a reality. By 2010, it was a pretty sure thing that the state would reach its very ambitious 20 percent goal early. So the CEC recommended a 33 percent renewable goal for the state by 2020. By 2015 it was clear that goal would also be achieved and

Governor Brown proposed a 50 percent renewables target by 2030. Focusing a powerful agency on long-term goals definitely pays off.

Under the federal PURPA, a state's public utility commission or the equivalent had the duty of determining a utility's avoided, or marginal, cost of production. This determination fell to the PUC in California and, of course, became very controversial. If the PUC used a formula that set the avoided cost low, as the utilities wanted, it would effectively kill the small renewable producers; they couldn't afford to build and operate new renewable technology at the cost of old, established fossil fuel plants. On the other hand, if the PUC set the avoided cost at a renewable replacement level, the renewable projects would pour in. The utilities would have to pay top dollar for the new technologies, and consumer rates could go up.

In the end, the PUC opted for contracts that paid enough to encourage new development of renewable power. The market responded positively to this and over 5,500 megawatts of new renewable generation were constructed. In total, when all the renewable energy standard offers were tabulated, and including some non-standard contracts, over 10,000 megawatts came on line, almost 15 percent of the state's needs.[92] Wind, solar thermal, geothermal, and biomass projects sprang up throughout California, and the state was seen as the vanguard of leadership to a large renewable energy future.

Of course, there was much controversy over the new programs and the resources devoted to them. The new renewable energy industry was happy; the utilities were not. What was happening was the progressive diminishment of the role of the utilities and the transfer to other energy producers, as well as to state government, of many of their prior functions. To some, the public interest was being enhanced, while to others, government intrusion was unwarranted and difficult to accept. But, as the 1970s came to a close, the shift in power and responsibilities from private companies to the public sector was pronounced.

To cement the new policy directions and to move them forward, Governor Brown sought change at the PUC and made his first two appointments in early 1975. His appointees were Leonard Ross, who early in life had won top honors on the television quiz show "The $64,000 Question," and Robert Batinovich, an accomplished businessman from San Mateo County. [93] Both viewed the utility industry as hidebound and in need of change. They wanted to continue the development of renewables and add increased emphasis on energy efficiency. In a 1975 decision, Ross and Batinovich set forth, in clear and convincing prose, the case for energy efficiency/conservation:

> "We regard conservation as the most important task facing utilities today. Continued growth of energy consumption at the rates we have known in the past would mean even higher rates for customers, multibillion dollar capital requirements for utilities, and unchecked proliferation of power plants. ... Reducing energy growth in an orderly, intelligent manner is the only long-term solution ...
>
> The effort we expect is not limited to exhortation, advertising, and traditional means of promoting conservation. We expect utilities to explore all possible cost-effective means of conservation, including intensive advisory programs directed at large customers, conservation-oriented research and development, [and] subsidy programs for capital-intensive conservation measures."[94]

The CEC had articulated the need for a new energy paradigm that included prioritizing energy efficiency. To make the goal a reality, in 1981 the PUC, under the leadership of President John Bryson (later to head Edison International), eventually "decoupled" the sale of electricity from its direct link to utility revenues, a revolutionary step. In other words, a utility's profits were no longer tied to how much electricity it sold. This encouraged utilities to be more supportive of energy efficiency and renewables, as their profits were now tied into performance goals supporting growth in these two areas.[95]

For the past 35 years, California utilities have had incentives to provide and encourage residential insulation, efficient appliances, energy audits, and renewable energy. This decoupling helped to reduce future growth in electricity demand from a compound growth rate of six percent to seven percent per year to a much lower rate of two percent a year. This means that today, Californians use only 55 percent of electricity per capita of the average American household. Yet since 1981, only a handful of other states have effectively decoupled utility revenues from sales.[96] The US energy efficiency numbers tell the tale of foregoing that policy solution.

Although in general, the California electric utilities dragged their feet on these changes, Southern California Edison enthusiastically endorsed the movement away from conventional generation to renewables. In 1980, Edison CEO William "Bill" Gould announced that the company was in support of the development of renewable and alternative energy resources. Its corporate plan focused on increased energy from wind, solar, geothermal, small hydro, fuel cells, cogeneration, and synthetic fuels. About 2,000 megawatts of new capacity ultimately came from these resources. Notable was the development, with the Luz Corporation, of 350 megawatts of parabolic trough central-station solar in the Mojave Desert, as well as geothermal energy. Edison also built the Solar One power tower, a concentrated, experimental 10-megawatt project, and the Cool Water Coal Gasification Plant to convert dirty coal into the much cleaner equivalent of natural gas. [97] [98]

Edison later planned to meet some of its expected load growth from two new out-of-state coal plants, Kaiparowits in Utah and Harry Allen-Warner Valley in Nevada, as well as the San Onofre Nuclear Generating Station units 2 and 3, and its partial ownership of the Palo Verde Nuclear Generation Station units in Arizona. Neither of the coal plants was built, and the San Onofre nuclear plant is now shut down.

In the case of the proposed coal plant in Utah, the opposition was led by local homeowner and movie star Robert Redford. His Sundance Film Festival in Park City is the largest independent film festival in the nation. The recriminations between Redford and Edison's then-President Howard Allen at one time reached fever pitch. Redford sent Allen a package in the midst of it. Edison security people refused to let him open it because it rattled suspiciously. It turned out to be a Christmas gift from Redford to Allen: a dried red-chili wreath, with some loose seeds in the chilies creating a small sound effect when moved.[99]

The energy efficiency work and the move to renewable power were really in support of what was always the biggest environmental policy arena in California—air quality—and all that is needed to be done statewide and regionally to improve it. With the CEC and PUC addressing stationary sources of pollution successfully, attention again turned to transportation sources, where the ARB was the undisputed leader.

The campaign manager of Brown's 1974 gubernatorial campaign was Tom Quinn, CEO of City News Service Inc., of Los Angeles. After Brown's victory, Quinn chose to join the new state administration in Sacramento as chair of the California Air Resources Board and as the secretary of environmental quality in the governor's cabinet. He was an outspoken advocate for cleaner air and used his position to push automobile manufacturers to equip their cars with two-way catalytic converters. In this, he built on the work of his predecessor, Reagan-appointee Dr. Arie J. Haagan-Smit. The ARB and regional air quality boards were aggressive in combating air pollution and saw the link between energy policy and the burning of high and then low sulfur fuel in power plants. In 1969, the ARB had set standards for various pollutants, such as photochemical oxidants, sulfur dioxide, nitrogen dioxide, and carbon monoxide. Two years later, it adopted the nation's first NO_x standards for automobiles.

During Quinn's four years at ARB, more aggressive regulatory programs were adopted. He set the tone and thrust of the agency, which has combated air pollution from vehicles, stationary sources, and agriculture ever since.[100] The ARB's "new sheriff in town" persona was solidified when Quinn stepped down in 1979 and was succeeded by his deputy, Mary Nichols, who went on to serve as the ARB chair through 1982. She returned to state government as secretary of the California Natural Resources Agency when Democrat Gray Davis was elected governor in 1998. After a hiatus following Davis's recall in 2003, she was again appointed head of ARB by Governor Schwarzenegger in 2007. She has remained in this position under Governor Brown. Nichols has been a linchpin in all of California's efforts in the air quality arena.

Profiles In Leadership

Senators Dianne Feinstein and Barbara Boxer and former Assembly Speaker and San Francisco Mayor Willie L. Brown Jr. built the bedrock of California's environmental success over many years. Many other people have been invaluable in specific areas of progress; some of them are profiled in this book.

Ralph Cavanagh—Natural Resources Defense Council

Courtesy of Ralph
Cavanagh

Ralph Cavanagh has the zeal of a missionary and the persistence of a badger. A fixture on the West Coast energy scene for more than thirty-five years, he is an issue-oriented advocate and a spellbinding speaker. A Yale Law School graduate, he is co-director of the Energy Program of the NRDC, a premier national environmental nongovernmental organization. He has shaped energy policy from the NRDC's San Francisco office, as visiting professor of law at Stanford and UC Berkeley and through his membership on many advisory boards.

Early on, Cavanagh showed a unique ability to work with utility companies and state regulators to achieve major energy efficiency improvements without hurting the economy. The NRDC approach has always been to make major changes behind the scenes to improve the environment through inventive policies that evolve into practice and law.

Perhaps his most impressive feat was helping institute utility "revenue decoupling," implemented in California by the Public Utilities Commission for electricity in 1981 and for natural gas in the late 1970s. Decoupling provides utilities with make-up revenues that they otherwise would lose through reduced sales caused by energy efficiency programs. In short, it allows utilities to recover revenues when their customers reduce usage because of energy efficiency. This is done by trueing up their loss of sales in year two by increasing their revenues by the amount of loss in year one. Cavanagh later took the campaign nationwide, and at last count, decoupling is the policy for electric utilities in seventeen states and for natural gas utilities in twenty-two states.

He served on the board of directors of the California Clean Energy Fund (CalCEF), established as a condition of the 2003 PG&E bankruptcy settlement requiring $30 million be paid by PG&E shareholders to create the fund. Its purpose is to invest in high-tech startup companies in the PG&E service territory, creating new technologies and jobs. Through a Cavanagh-inspired California Clean Energy Fund challenge grant, in 2006 he helped establish the University of California, Davis Energy Efficiency Center, which focuses on transferring technology into the marketplace, creating jobs. It has inspired creation of similar centers, first at Stanford and now at four other universities.

Charles Hugh Warren—California Energy Commission

Courtesy of Charles
Hugh Warren

A bear of a man with a warm smile, Charlie Warren was an early political and environmental activist who thought California was on the wrong energy path and might end up building nuclear power plants all along its coast, when there was a better, more environmentally sound course of action.

Warren, a lawyer, legislator, and environmental leader, was born in 1927 in Kansas City, Missouri, and became a Californian after attending the University of California, Berkeley. He was chair of the San Francisco Young Democrats and moved to Southern California in 1955 to become part of the influential Los Angeles law firm of Bodle, Fogel and Warren.

Warren was elected to the California State Assembly in 1962. His early legislative interests included civil rights, air quality, and transportation, but he is best known as co-author of the 1974 Warren-Alquist Act, the legislation that created the California Energy Commission (CEC).

He was also the principal sponsor and author of the statute that made protection of the California coast a permanent feature of state life. He successfully sponsored the 1976 Nuclear Safeguards Act, which prohibits new nuclear plants from being built in California unless and until the federal government establishes permanent storage for high-level nuclear waste. This law is still in force, because the federal government has not yet provided nuclear waste storage facilities.

In 1976, Warren left the state legislature to join the Carter administration as chair of the President's Council on Environmental Quality. In this role, he promulgated agricultural land preservation, water resource development, and alternative energy systems in the California mode. Upon Carter's defeat by Ronald Reagan in 1980, Warren returned to California to continue his environmental leadership on the State Coastal Commission and then as director of the State Lands Commission, overseeing some of the oil industry's projects offshore and seeking to enhance the scenic Mono Lake on the east side of the Sierra Nevada mountain range.

Now in his early nineties, Warren lives in Sacramento. His many accomplishments and involvement in a broad range of issues are outlined in the "Inventory of the Charles Warren Papers" in the California State Archives and have been recorded in the oral history project of the Bancroft Library of the University of California, Berkeley.

William Richard Gould—Southern California Edison

© Fitzgerald Whitney 2001, Los Angeles Times

William "Bill" Gould, president and later chairman and CEO of Southern California Edison Company from 1978 through 1984, was a utility industry visionary. Gould, born in Provo, Utah, in 1919, earned a degree in mechanical engineering from the University of Utah and a graduate degree in naval architecture and marine engineering from Massachusetts Institute of Technology and Dartmouth College. After serving in the Navy, Gould joined Edison as a mechanical engineer and held several officer titles until he was promoted to the top position.

His signature project was building the Pacific DC Intertie, the 800-mile direct current (DC) line linking the Pacific Northwest with Southern California. The Intertie brought low-cost hydropower to millions of California customers. What sets Gould apart, however, was his embrace of new and decentralized sources of electric energy. In this he was alone in the electric utility industry, often considered "way out" and off base. Undeterred and recognizing early on that the utility industry was facing new challenges and a new environment, he set a strong vision for Edison. In doing so, he remarked, "If a species doesn't go through a mutation to meet its new environment, it doesn't survive. A corporation is in the same situation."

Edison relied on oil and gas to fuel 67 percent of its electricity production in 1973. After the 1973 Arab oil embargo, this reliance on fossil fuels caused sharp increases in electricity prices. A few years later, the company's "Planning for Uncertainty" report made note of Edison's October 1980 decision "to put its corporate resources behind the rapid development and deployment of renewable and alternative energy resource[s]," specifically wind, solar, geothermal, small hydro, fuel cells, cogeneration, and synthetic fuels. "About 2,000 megawatts of new capacity was to come from these renewable and alternative resources—the new flagship of the Edison Company. ..."

Under Gould's plan, one-third of the company's new generation in the 1980s would come from solar, geothermal, and wind power. And it did, making Edison the first large utility to rely on such an increase in non-hydro renewable resources. In recognition of Gould's vision and leadership, Edison in 1982 was the first cor- poration awarded the John & Alice Tyler Prize for Environmental Achievement.

Mary Nichols—California Air Resources Board

Courtesy of the
State of California,
Diana Miller
Photography

No one has done more to protect and enhance the California environment over the past forty years than Mary Nichols. Cleaning the air, changing the energy mix, prodding the automobile manufacturers, and battling the oil industry have all been in her long-term portfolio.

Nichols grew up in Ithaca, New York, where her father was a professor at Cornell University and later the Socialist mayor of Ithaca. She went to Cornell University, taking off the summer of 1964 to register voters in Mississippi. After graduation she became one of the first female journalists at The Wall Street Journal. *Then she headed to Yale to earn a law degree.*

On a road trip to Los Angeles, she was both horrified by the hideous and dense smog that left a chemical taste in her mouth and simultaneously entranced by the beauty of Southern California. She was struck by the color of the sky, describing it as "a peculiar, Day-Glo chemical kind of orange." In 1971, she moved to Los Angeles, her home ever since, with her husband, John Daum. She became a clean air litigator, seeking to improve Southern California's dirty, unsafe air.

Nichols's credentials led Governor Brown to appoint her to the ARB. She succeeded Tom Quinn in the full-time position of ARB chair in 1979, serving until 1983. Returning to Los Angeles from Sacramento, she spent the balance of the 1980s in several jobs—providing environmental law advice and managing Los Angeles Mayor Tom Bradley's second and unsuccessful run for governor in 1984. She led several nonprofits and founded the Los Angeles office of the Natural Resources Defense Council.

In 1992, she became an assistant administrator for the Environmental Protection Agency under President Clinton. In that position, she was responsible for implementing the nation's acid rain trading program, showing that a market-based system could be developed to reduce air pollution. Returning to Los Angeles, Governor Gray Davis soon asked her to serve as secretary of the California Natural Resources Agency.

She stepped down after Davis was recalled by voters and went back to Los Angeles as a professor of law at UCLA, where she became director of its Institute of the Environment. In 2007, she answered a call from Governor Arnold Schwarzenegger and his chief of staff, Susan Kennedy, to return to state government to again chair the ARB.

Every major California air quality initiative for the past twenty-five years has Mary Nichols's stamp on it. She helped ban lead in gasoline in the 1970s and is working to cut gasoline use in the state by half in a few years. She has ushered in the eras of methanol, then electric and now fuel-cell cars. She has led the fight against diesel emissions from the thousands of ships bringing goods to the United States through the gateway of California. She oversees the implementation of the state's cap-and-trade program, the most ambitious in the world. She is negotiating an extremely innovative plan with Volkswagen as the company attempts to mitigate its diesel scandal.

Nichols is strategic and tenacious. Perhaps her most important legacy will be her decades of mentoring hundreds of up-and-coming environmentalists to assure that the environmental ethic strengthens and perseveres in the next generation of leaders.

CHAPTER 5

THE BRIDE OF FRANKENSTEIN

It's a short road that has no bumps and curves. Nowhere was this more apparent than the detour California took when it decided to try a different path toward a new energy future—the path of relying mostly upon a competitive electricity market. It was a massive failure for reasons outlined in this chapter, and the consequences are still felt today. It stands at an object lesson in bad public policy. Even when followed with good intentions, a flawed direction can cause a whirlwind of trouble.

The California electric power crisis has had a major and lasting impact, first in terms of much higher electricity rates. It also changed the rationale and substance of many electricity regulatory policies and practices. The crisis hit its peak with rolling brownouts and massive rate increases in 2001 and 2002. The people of California had had it. In fall 2003, they recalled Governor Gray Davis over the debacle, and, in that same election, selected Arnold Schwarzenegger his successor.

The roots of the crisis go back to President Jimmy Carter and the 1978 Airline Deregulation Act. Before 1978, the government controlled which companies could fly in the United States, what they could charge, and where they could fly. After airline deregulation, many airline ticket prices plummeted under freer market conditions, and there were nearly a score of new companies in the industry. Competition, for a time, flourished. Heads nodded approvingly in Congress. Trains, telephones, and other monopolistic industries soon were loaded onto the deregulation bandwagon.

California was not immune to the interest in deregulation and the promotion of competition. In-state trucking, long regulated by the Public Utilities Commission (PUC), was deregulated. In-state airlines, most notably Pacific Southwest Airlines (PSA) and Air California (AirCal), were no longer regulated by the PUC. The bulls-eye was now electric utilities.

In 1990, Republican US Senator and former San Diego Mayor Pete Wilson was elected governor, defeating San Francisco Mayor Dianne Feinstein. Shortly thereafter, he made two appointments to the PUC. The most notable was Daniel Fessler, a law professor at the University of California, Davis. Fessler, a balding Anglophile, affected a faint-ly British accent, though born and raised in Wyoming. A brilliant iconoclast, he was passionate about the concept of free markets. He also was determined to follow Margaret Thatcher's United Kingdom down the path to electricity deregulation.[101] Britain portrayed itself on posters advertising electricity deregulation as Frankenstein break-ing his chains and escaping electrocution. Fessler began to create the California Bride of Frankenstein.

Fessler was taken with the breakup of the monopolized British electrical system and the introduction of competitive markets. To him, the bible on how and why to deregulate the electric market was Lord Parkinson's *Right at the Centre: An Autobiography*. After a trip to London to learn about the British experiment first-hand, accom-panied by industry representatives, state legislators, and his fellow commissioner, Gregory Conlon, Fessler returned to California deter-mined to revamp the California electricity market. This bore fruit in the publication *The Blue Book*, in which Fessler, Conlon, and some senior staff set forth a new deregulated and competitive future.[102]

The proposals in *The Blue Book* and its subsequent iterations were viewed with varying degrees of horror by most of the regular partici-pants at the PUC.[103] The utilities saw the breakup of their longtime monopoly. Environmental organizations felt the new thrust might di-minish the policy emphasis on energy efficiency and the development of new, alternative generating technologies, such as wind and solar. Labor and consumer groups saw the rules under which they could successfully navigate go up in smoke. Policymakers in interested gov-ernment agencies, always uneasy with the prospect of rapid change, weighed in on the side of caution and deliberation. On the flip side, independent power producers and their bankers saw opportunity.

All this angst meant that the truly bold move of deregulating the state electricity industry and introducing widespread competition was too big a step for the PUC alone to take. Instead, all the major parties, including the PUC, turned to the California legislature for resolution. No one at the time truly understood what a fateful decision deregulation was, including the legislature itself, which proceeded with vigor to seek a resolution to the challenge of introducing full-fledged competition in the electrical sector, while trying to protect or placate all the players from any undesirable consequences.

All the interested parties—the utilities, the independent power producers, the unions, consumer groups, local governments, environmental organizations, the PUC, other state government bodies, and the governor's office—rushed to Sacramento to describe their hopes and fears. It was an amazing display, with lobbyists of all persuasions hoping to be retained to help shape any legislation.[104]

To the surprise of many, an overarching compromise did ultimately emerge, steered by the political skills of Republican Assemblyman Jim Brulte, the nominal author of the legislation, and the adroitness of Democratic state Senator Steve Peace, a former movie producer of the cult favorite *Attack of the Killer Tomatoes*. Peace oversaw the details, big and small, of the legislation, AB 1890, which bore Brulte's name.[105]

The final bill, which was passed unanimously by the legislature and signed into law by Governor Pete Wilson, was a work of art. Every major interest group and player got something, though it is fair to say the utilities got the least and gave the most.

The utilities were stripped of their near-monopoly status as the ultimate legislation provided for a competitive, open market. Any new electricity provider could compete for and win over those customers who had only known one utility service their entire lives. This was the brave new world of retail competition, effective March 31, 1998.[106] Moreover, the utilities were, by law, forced to sell almost all of their conventional gas-fired generation, keeping basically only their hydroelectric and nuclear generating units.[107] They were compensated, however, for their losses through the imposition of a Competitive Transition Charge (CTC), to be paid for years to come by all customers. The CTC spared the electric utilities the fate of the local telephone utilities that preceded them, which had been forced to write off without compensation much of their plant and equipment when they entered a competitive market.

The electric utilities retained ownership but lost control of their high-voltage transmission network, which spanned the state north to south and east to west. In fact, one of the most far-reaching outcomes of AB 1890 was the legislature's and the governor's willingness to cede regulatory control over the utilities' transmission systems to a federal agency, the Federal Energy Regulatory Commission (FERC) in Washington, D.C. This transfer of authority was unprecedented and permanent, for as more than one wag noted, "You give something to the feds and you can kiss it goodbye forever."

The legislation also created another new entity, the Power Exchange, whose job was to purchase power and balance the power needs of customers on the spot- and day-ahead market.[108] The utilities were required to forego their historic role of unilateral purchaser of bulk power in favor of buying power from competitive generators, including companies that now owned and operated the gas-fired generation the utilities were forced to sell. But, to keep the overall electrical grid in balance each minute of each day, it was believed that some organization would need to balance the system's constantly altering supply and demand. Hence, the Power Exchange.

In total, these changes were historic for electric utilities. They no longer could be assured of their customer base, they could no longer build new, conventional power plants and they could no longer solely run their still-owned high-voltage transmission system. A revolution had occurred, though few at the time grasped its nature or lasting impact.

The independent energy producers, particularly those wishing to build or buy conventional gas-fired plants, were advantaged by AB 1890. The two biggest utilities, PG&E and Southern California Edison, were forced to sell their gas generators. And a new set of companies came on the scene. Most of Edison's coastal generating units were purchased by the AES Corporation and NRG Energy Inc., and new players, such as Mirant Corp. and Duke Energy, bought PG&E's generators.[109] All of a sudden, the electricity industry in California greatly increased in size. With many new players came many new voices in Sacramento.

The unions, consumer, and environmental groups got little from the legislation, though each claimed they were part of the grand compromise and were on board as the bill made its way to the governor's desk.

Among the many governmental agencies, the PUC was the most affected. Its longtime regulatory role over monopoly utilities was significantly diminished. This was the second major chipping away of PUC power. Twenty-two years previously, the California Energy Commission had been created and took over major responsibilities.

In the summer of 1996, Governor Wilson, pronouncing himself pleased, signed AB 1890 into law, with the effective date for full implementation of the new competitive market set for March 31, 1998. The bill was truly a bipartisan exercise. While not a single legislator voted no, a few years later, many would publicly express regret for their vote. Even liberal icons, such as legendary Democratic state Senator John Burton of San Francisco, voted yes.

––––––––

Throughout fall 1996 and all of 1997, a host of new market entrants and several affiliates of out-of-state utilities sought to position themselves for the soon-to-be competitive future. Contracts were signed and deals were made as the implementation date loomed. Overnight, customers began to leave the utilities for new energy providers. It did not take long for a groundswell to emerge, as customers large and small signed contracts with the new suppliers.

The utilities worked to stem the flow, often acting anti-competitively and drawing out the process by which a customer could leave them for a new provider. Each time a utility customer sought a new supplier, the utilities employed various stratagems to slow the process of change, a rearguard and ultimately unsuccessful effort to thwart what was to become known as "direct access."

By the end of the first full year of retail competition, Southern California Edison had lost nearly 13 percent of its retail sales. PG&E and San Diego Gas & Electric experienced similar losses. The University of California, partnered with the California State University system, picked Enron to be its new statewide electricity provider, a choice that proved ill-fated a few years later when Enron was found to be illegally manipulating the system. The company raked in billions but went bankrupt.

Ralph's grocery chain, with 100 megawatts of load, chose a start-up company, New Energy Ventures (NEV), (co-founded by this book's co-author, Michael Peevey), as did the US Department of Defense, which shifted its entire electricity load from the three investor-owned utilities to NEV.[110] [111] In Northern California, Safeway Stores left PG&E for a new supplier, as did the municipal load of California's third largest city, San Jose.[112] At the residential level, thousands of homeowners forsook their local utilities for new suppliers who represented their products as far "greener" than that of the utilities.[113]

New Energy Ventures provides a good illustration of how an independent energy provider could go from startup with no revenue to a $700 million company in eighteen months in the new deregulated marketplace. By 1995, when the drums began to beat for energy deregulation in California, Peevey—having served in labor, nonprofit, and for-profit businesses associated with energy, most recently as president of Southern California Edison—was well positioned to understand the emerging business advantages for an independent energy provider. He and colleague Michael Burke formed NEV early that year. Their business model was to become one of the new "direct access" power providers created by deregulation's passage in 1996.

Initial funding was provided by Tucson Electric Power, which committed several million dollars over three years. Early on, NEV officials decided the company would seek to be a direct access provider principally to commercial, industrial, and government entities, leaving the residential market to others. They opened offices in Boston, New York, Philadelphia, and Chicago and grew from three employees in 1995 to 300 by 1998, the year deregulation was fully implemented.

The company had to secure a source of power that would allow it to offer prices below the utilities' as well as a growing number of independent competitors. They found it at the federal Bonneville Power Administration in the Pacific Northwest, which had a surplus, due to a decline in demand by its large direct-service industries, such as aluminum. Bonneville offered NEV an option to buy up to 441 megawatts of power over 4.5 years at a leveled price of 3.8 cents per kilowatt hour, which was lower than the going market rate in California, even before the frenzy of market manipulation occurred in 2001 to 2002.

No other free market competitor enjoyed the advantage of having BPA as a multiple-year supplier at a very attractive price.

With this contract in hand, NEV was able to sign sales contracts with many large users, including the US Department of Defense, Macy's, California Steel, Grimmway Farms, and many local governments. The company was supplying more than 1,000 megawatts of electricity to its California customers and was also having success elsewhere, including New York, where most of the premier hotels, along with the United Nations complex, became customers. In a few years it had become one of the largest energy-service suppliers in the nation.

The rapid growth, from zero revenue in early 1998 to more than $700 million in 1999, had a serious downside. In keeping up with the electric supply needed for all the new customers, NEV's credit requirements soon rose to more than $100 million. As a nod to its new view of itself as no longer a startup, the company changed its name to New Energy (NE).

Still, the cost of borrowing was eating all of NE's potential profits. The company realized it couldn't finance its own tremendous headlong growth, and in the summer of 1999, NE sold itself to AES, a large independent power producer with offices around the world, for $92 million. New Energy later was sold by AES to Baltimore Gas and Electric Company, which itself was acquired by Exelon, a large Chicago-based utility. Today, NE is part of the Exelon family of companies and is considered to be the nation's largest energy-service provider. It would have a market capitalization of more than $2 billion if it were a stand-alone company.

————

So it went, from 1998 well into 2000. There were new electricity suppliers, competing with one another as well as seeking utility customers. There were many new generators selling their product to the new energy-service companies. There were the investor-owned utilities, backpedaling as they lost customers and feeling their best days had passed. In terms of overall state policy, "the genius of the market"—the claim made for deregulation—was going strong. Of course, there was a sizeable downside: commitments to energy efficiency by both regulators at the PUC and the utilities were greatly diminished.

Likewise, investments in new or improved technologies, such as wind, solar, and fuels cells fell sharply. Some observers and participants began to lament the decline in support for technological change and innovation that had marked California public policy in prior years.

Then, suddenly, it seemed, this big new policy thrust in favor of less government intervention in the marketplace, which was being duplicated in such states as Massachusetts, New York, Pennsylvania, Texas, and Illinois, began to weaken, then falter and collapse, at least in California. What had happened?

It began in San Diego, when the local utility became the first utility, in late spring 2000, to be cut loose from much of the transition regulation stemming from passage of AB 1890.[114] Freed of much regulation and dependent on the vagaries of an open, free market, SDG&E began to see sharp and sustained electricity price increases.[115] They were clearly the result of market manipulation and gaming of the system by in-state and out-of-state electricity producers, sellers, and marketers.[116] Yet SDG&E could not raise retail rates to respond to their new costs because, although supply pricing was now deregulated, retail price regulation under the PUC continued. As expected in such a scenario, SDG&E began to acquire considerable debt in the form of ever-more costly wholesale power purchases.[117]

At first, the situation of high wholesale costs and frozen retail rates was confined to San Diego, a condition that lasted through much of summer 2000. The San Diego utility was in a real bind financially. It sought relief by securing legislative passage in Sacramento of a bill that provided it with a state-guaranteed IOU that eventually they would be made financially whole. Despite such help and other efforts, it soon became clear that the San Diego experience would not remain a regional or even a state concern for long. Like a cancer, what happened in San Diego spread. And it was out of California's control.

Wholesale price regulation had been willingly given by the state to the FERC under deregulation.[118] Therefore, price limits had to be imposed by the federal government. But the FERC believed in the sanctity of competitive markets. And helping out California after stupid mistakes was not its highest priority. The state was rebuffed; the FERC looked the other way, spurning requests that grew in intensity and scope as 2000 progressed.[119] The state was now entering the beginning of the California energy crisis, a crisis that would create havoc with some, heavy economic costs for all, and a lasting legacy.

By late summer 2000, it was becoming clear that the two biggest utilities, PG&E and Southern California Edison, were also getting into a deep hole. The wholesale price of electricity in the state continued to soar, and retail rates, set by the PUC, were frozen. As more than one observer noted, "This is a recipe for disaster. We need either price controls by the FERC or rate increases by the PUC."

In September, the utilities tried a different avenue to save themselves. Because they no longer owned most of their own generation plants, they went to the PUC, hat in hand, and asked permission to enter into multi-year contracts with some electricity suppliers. Some of the wholesalers were interested, because it would lock in their sales for a defined period, and they were willing to trade lower prices for their commodity for the security of a certain level of sales. But, of course, no one could be certain that the price the buyers and sellers agreed upon would be lower than the competitive market price in the short-term market.

Now it was up to the PUC. Should it encourage the utilities to "go long" on a portion of their electricity demand, or should it simply say no, sticking with its proclamation that reliance on the competitive market is the right course?

The PUC basically did neither. Instead, it told the utilities they could "go long" and sign multi-year power purchases, but they would be subject to after-the-fact reasonableness reviews of their decisions. In other words, they were given not a green light, but an amber one. The PUC essentially said, "Go ahead, but we reserve the right to second-guess you. If we find later that you spent too much for the power today, you will be disallowed cost recovery." The PUC had a history of after-the-fact reasonableness reviews, which was fairly standard practice in utility regulation. Most times, utility imprudence led to modest disallowances, but there were occasions when some were very large, running into the tens of millions of dollars. After much hand-wringing on whether to take on such downside risk, the utilities said, "No thanks." That's when the California energy crisis began in earnest.

The five PUC commissioners were President Loretta Lynch, Carl Wood, Henry M. Duque, Richard A. Bilas, and Josiah L. Neeper.[120] The first two were appointees of Governor Gray Davis, while the others had been appointed by former Governor Pete Wilson.

Lynch was a longtime political operative, active in the campaigns of many prominent Democrats, including Bill Clinton in his first run for president in 1992, US Senator Dianne Feinstein in her first race for her seat, and Gray Davis in his campaign for governor in 1998. She had no background or knowledge of the energy industry upon her appointment in March 2000. Her ally on the PUC was Carl Wood, also appointed by Davis only a few months earlier, after a career as the head of the Utility Workers Union of America local at Southern California Edison's San Onofre Nuclear Generating Station.

Why weren't the three Wilson appointees, a voting majority, not assertive as the first year of the energy crisis progressed? Certainly there was good reason to be, with wholesale prices in the state increasing 800 percent between April and December 2000.

The skyrocketing prices were aided by the increasingly widespread market manipulation by a growing number of sellers, particularly Enron, whose price-gouging schemes were given colorful names, such as "Ricochet" and "Fat Boy."[121] With prices up and retail rates frozen by the PUC, the utilities reached out to friends and allies, but to no avail. They pleaded with Lynch and her staff to support a rate increase, again to no avail. It was clear that Lynch was looking to the governor's office for a sign of what to do. None was forthcoming.

Finally, Warren Christopher, a noted statesman and respected thought leader who had served as secretary of state in Bill Clinton's first presidential term, sat down with the governor.[122] At the meeting, Christopher urged Davis to assume leadership, citing how Clinton, during the Mexican debt crisis a few years earlier, had acted boldly, even risking his presidency, to rescue Mexico from financial collapse. Christopher said that this is what leadership is all about, to do the right thing, even if the political risks are large. Davis was not swayed. He was afraid of the political backlash from raising consumer utility rates enough to cover the rising wholesale prices.

The meeting ended with no agreement, and the energy crisis, already in process, went to full throttle. By the end of 2000 the situation, by common agreement, was in chaos. Power shortages, brownouts, and blackouts began.[123] The utilities were fast running out of money to pay their bills. Retail rates remained frozen, except for some slight relief in December, while wholesale rates were at historic heights.

GUARDS AT THE FRONT LOBBY OF THE CALIFORNIA PUBLIC UTILITIES COMMISSION BUILDING AFTER IT WAS HIT BY ROLLING BLACKOUTS.
Courtesy of the Associated Press

The governor went to Washington, D.C., in December 2000 to seek intervention by the Clinton administration in its waning days.[124] He met with Treasury Secretary Larry Summers in his boardroom with Federal Reserve Chairman Alan Greenspan, Energy Secretary Bill Richardson, Enron CEO Ken Lay, and SoCal Edison CEO John Bryson, among others, including Warren Christopher.[125] But he was turned down; he was told that California should solve its own problems by increasing retail rates. [126] Davis had two Republican and two Democratic state legislators with him, and they all rejected that suggestion.[127] Through the holiday season and into the new year, the crisis worsened. [128]

The utilities were in a situation where they could no longer buy the electricity their customers needed. They were broke, and no lender would step forward to help. Widespread blackouts were imminent, and the state was forced to enter the breech, with its full faith and credit. The California Department of Water Resources, with the state's credit behind it, began to buy electricity for the utilities, doing what is called "sleeving," using its financial strength to guarantee the utilities' power needs.[129]

————————

As 2001 began, California had skyrocketing wholesale electricity prices, and most sellers of electricity were manipulating the market. California utilities were such an easy mark that even government bodies, such as the Los Angeles Department of Water and Power, BC Hydro and the federal Bonneville Power Administration couldn't resist the opportunity to price gouge.[130]   There were periodic power shortages, causing brownouts. The utilities were not credit worthy, and talk of their possible bankruptcy began. Still, the PUC, with one new member, former San Francisco Public Defender Geoffrey Brown, who replaced Neeper, did not act to raise rates.[131] Instead, Lynch continued to look for a signal from the governor. None came.

The crisis intensified in January. In mid-month, Lynn Schenk, the governor's chief of staff, called Michael Peevey and asked him to come to Sacramento and help.[132] He did, working as a volunteer out of a small office in the "horseshoe" (both the shape and the informal name of the California governor's offices) for the next two months. S. David Freeman, general manager of the Los Angeles Department of Water and Power, who had taken a leave to help the state, soon joined him.[133] Vikram Budhraja, consultant and former head of policy and planning at Edison, and Larry Hamlin, head of power supply at Edison, were recruited by Peevey to help out, as was Randy Hardy, former head of the federal Bonneville Power Administration.[134]

There were crisis meetings daily, often from dawn to well into the night. Daily morning meetings with the governor were a staple. He would phone in from his residence, often commenting while riding his exercise bike. Within the governor's office there were many participants, all articulating their perspectives on what should be done. The rock was Susan Kennedy, the cabinet secretary. Unruffled, quick and decisive, she was a constant in a muddled and often chaotic operation.

In the legislature, the leadership was deeply involved in seeking solutions, though without knowing whether its remedies were workable. Assembly Speaker Bob Hertzberg understood that fundamentals of the problem turned partly around money and sought the help of investment bankers to structure a solution for the state.[135] These efforts often floundered in the face of the governor's continued opposition to rate increases.

An example of the wild and chaotic events in early 2001 can be gleaned from a single episode. One evening, the governor called yet another meeting of major players and advisers, both in and out of state government. The participants included investment bankers from Wall Street who had been trying to help structure assistance for California. As everyone filed into the meeting room, it became apparent that an earlier meeting was just ending.

The governor sat at his big conference table with the powerful Senate President *Pro Tem* John Burton on his left. As people were settling into their chairs, Burton suddenly stood up, said to the governor, "On top of everything else you are a fucking incompetent," and stormed out. [136]

The room went deathly quiet. Hertzberg ran to bring Burton back. He returned a few minutes later and said, "Burton's not coming back, maybe ever." The meeting proceeded for a couple of minutes and broke up. The investment bankers and other participants from out of state could not believe California state government officials could behave in such a way. Subsequently, the state's cost of money from bankers increased.

Though often rough talking, outlandish in behavior, and given to sprinkling his ordinary conversation with plenty of blue words, Burton worked hard to find solutions.[137] The state was in a deep crisis, and the two biggest utilities were on the verge of bankruptcy. They needed some rate relief. Still, Governor Davis would not act, and without him, neither would PUC President Lynch.

Burton's favorite line was, "I want a hot dog for a dollar," meaning he wasn't willing to pay extortion rates for electricity contracts. So he proposed the state take ownership of the utilities' high-voltage transmission system, a proposal rejected by most all concerned. Next, he suggested the state go into the power plant business.

This was more successful and led to the passage of legislation creating the California Consumer Power and Conservation Financing Authority, whose mission was to finance new generation capacity and assure stability in the state's electrical supply. It eventually was led by S. David Freeman. A few years later, Arnold Schwarzenegger became governor. In his campaign, he promised to "blow up the boxes," claiming there were too many state agencies.[138] He blew up only one agency—the Power Authority.

Peevey and Michael Khan, a San Francisco lawyer and ardent Davis supporter, met with the utilities nearly daily.[139] Freeman and consultant Budhraja took up residence in the governor's Los Angeles office and began to negotiate long-term power purchase contracts between generators and the state Department of Water Resources, which had, as noted earlier, begun to "sleeve" for the utilities.[140]

Over several weeks, the Freeman-Budhraja team, aided by consultants from Navigant Consulting, successfully negotiated contracts for thousands of megawatts of power, thereby significantly reducing both volatility in the marketplace and the widespread manipulation that was occurring.[141] They never signed a contract with Enron, despite repeated efforts by CEO Ken Lay, because the price was too high.

Much of this was summarized in a report written in early March 2001 for Governor Davis by Peevey, Freeman, and Budhraja and discussed with him. In addition to the power purchases, the team made a series of recommendations, including abolishing the Power Exchange and the Electricity Oversight Board. (**See condensed report – Appendix I**)

The report was particularly critical of the PUC, noting: "It is important to point out that the CPUC as currently structured and operating is dysfunctional and requires substantial overhaul to make it responsive to meeting State energy policy needs. State's current shortages in power supplies, transmission bottlenecks, gas pipeline bottlenecks, lack of in-state gas storage can to a large part be traced to CPUC decisions over the last 15 to 20 years. CPUC must be altered in terms of its focus, leadership, staffing, and size."

Further, the report noted that the FERC's lifting of price caps on short-term gas pipeline capacity had been an unmitigated disaster, saying, "California has been rendered a deep wound, which doesn't need to bleed anymore to prove itself fatal."

Resumption of the price caps did take place later in 2001, under the leadership of new FERC Chairman Pat Wood of Texas.[142] New long-term negotiated contracts, coupled with the decision in summer of 2001 by the FERC to place meaningful price caps on wholesale power markets, finally helped end the energy crisis, though the after-effects would play out for years.[143] [144]

Eventually, a series of actions brought a "new normal" to California's electric market. As usual, the people in the state get big credit. As rolling brownouts (which were feared might turn to full blackouts) continued in the hot summer of 2001, a group of utility experts the governor assembled to guide him proposed a new state "20/20 Program,"[145] which asked residential users to cut their electricity use by 20 percent over the summer months[146] in return for a 20 percent bill credit; in addition, they would save money through the 20 percent usage reduction.[147]

Governor Davis endorsed the proposal and conveyed his wishes to the PUC, which adopted it. The program was a great success, with one-third of all utility residential consumers reducing their usage by 20 percent or more.[148] Another one-third reduced their usage, but did not reach the 20 percent target. Pleased with this, the PUC ultimately extended the program into the summers of 2002 and 2003 and essentially coupled with the Flex Your Power program to reduce electricity consumption when needed statewide.

Meanwhile, legislation was enacted that set many terms and conditions for dealing with the energy crisis, including suspension of the direct-access rules, which had allowed customers to switch to independent power providers in the first place. [149] At Burton's insistence, a rate freeze for small-energy-use consumers was included.

———

Still, the effects of the crisis lingered. Something had to give, and it finally did. The governor, after opposing any significant rate increases for nine months, finally accepted the inevitable, recognizing the utilities could not be viable companies with a continued huge disparity between their wholesale power costs and their retail rates as set by the PUC.[150]

With the governor's support,[151] the PUC in May 2001 allowed the utilities to increase their retail rates by 30 percent all at once. The state adopted a multi-tiered retail rate structure, with those who used the most electricity paying much higher rates for greater usage, up to 71 percent more for SoCal Edison customers and 80 percent for PG&E customers.[152] [153] The many-tiered rate system, with some modifications, has remained in place ever since.[154]

PG&E had decided it could no longer operate under the state's regulatory system and declared in April 2001 that it was filing for bankruptcy.[155] This action was a body blow to the state, making California appear unable to take care of itself and, of course, caused an outpouring of editorials by *The Wall Street Journal* and others proclaiming the state government irresponsible.[156] In fact, while PG&E was extremely unhappy with what it perceived as unreasonable, unfair, and biased regulatory behavior by the PUC, there were other factors at play.

Utilities had been treated badly throughout the energy crisis, and it was time to fight back. If PG&E went bankrupt, it might allow its 4,000 megawatts of regulatory-based hydro assets to be sold at market pricing rather than depreciated value. Through bankruptcy, which would play out in federal bankruptcy court, PG&E sought to become, for its hydro assets, a FERC-, not a PUC-, regulated entity.[157] In short, the utility wished to make a jailbreak from California regulation and be under the FERC umbrella. The PG&E management believed this would mean greatly increased earnings for the company.[158] Customer rate increases would help insure that profit.

The utility's bankruptcy filing and the likelihood that Edison also would file for bankruptcy was a radical move, and it came as a shock.[159] Political leaders panicked, which led to the 30 percent rate increase mentioned earlier.[160] The state, through the PUC, fought PG&E in the federal courts for the next thirty-plus months, until a federal bankruptcy judge urged a settlement.[161]

The company abandoned its effort to jump from PUC to FERC regulation of its hydro assets. It further agreed to cede control of more than 140,000 acres of Sierra Nevada mountain land surrounding its hydro facilities to a newly created nonprofit organization, the Pacific Forest and Watershed Lands Stewardship Council, in perpetuity, thereby ensuring that never again could it contemplate having the pricing of its hydro system under the FERC.[162]

Also, again in a very California fashion that emphasized technology as the bright light at the end of every tunnel, PG&E agreed to fund, with $30 million of shareholder money, the California Clean Energy Fund.[163] Its purpose was to make investments in high-technology startup companies in the PG&E service territory.[164] At the end of 2003, the PUC, by a vote of 3 to 2, approved the settlement, stimulated by the peacemaking efforts of a federal bankruptcy judge.[165]

After PG&E had declared bankruptcy in 2001, Edison was also nearly out of money and credit.[166] Politicians were extremely concerned that the state's two largest energy utilities could be in bankruptcy, fearing, with some logic, that people would believe the state was out of control and unmanageable. The 30 percent rate increase was intended in part to prevent Edison from also filing for bankruptcy and to give investors and citizens some sense that the state knew what it was doing.

As a price of not declaring bankruptcy, Edison also negotiated with the PUC that its wholesale rate increases could be passed on to customers from now on, and that the company could also collect the wholesale price increases totaling more than $3 billion that it had to swallow during the energy crisis.[167] This agreement stemmed from a lawsuit Edison had earlier brought against the PUC, claiming that the so-called "filed rate doctrine," a principle of regulatory law, required the PUC to pass along to Edison customers the wholesale price increases it was paying.[168] The PUC had refused.

The bankruptcy threat was a game changer, however, and the PUC and the company negotiated a compromise whereby Edison would get the money it claimed it was owed under the doctrine by passing along to its customers the more than $3 billion, minus a $300 million disallowance.[169]

The commissioners approved the settlement[170] without public hearings, which was not only unusual, but unprecedented. The Utility Reform Network (TURN) challenged the action in the state Supreme Court but lost when the court denied review.[171] The Edison-PUC settlement brought a sigh of relief in many quarters. Shortly thereafter, the governor appointed Peevey to the PUC to fill the expired term of Commissioner Bilas, who resigned.[172] [173] With thousands of megawatts of new long-term power purchase contracts and the imposition of some price caps by FERC, the Edison settlement, the approval of a very large rate increase by the PUC, and the appointment of new commissioners, there was a growing feeling that the worst was over, that the crisis was now manageable, and it would end. It did, though effects and consequences, as well as lessons learned, continue to this day.

Profiles in Leadership
Susan Kennedy—Chief Aide to Governors Gray Davis and Arnold Schwarzenegger

© Robert Durell

Few match Susan Kennedy in energy, determination, drive, and outcomes. Her ultra-competitive nature played out in one paintball war among the Schwarzenegger staff. She tore a knee ligament, but wouldn't go to the hospital until the game was won. "That's Susan through and through," commented a staffer.

A native of Rumson, New Jersey, Kennedy graduated with honors from Saint Mary's College of California in Moraga with a degree in management. She began her life as a political activist when she moved to Los Angeles. Kennedy worked on environmental issues tenants' rights, and other such causes.

Her leadership from 1991 to 1995 as executive director of the state Democratic Party earned high marks from Democratic politicians and led to her becoming communications director for US Senator Dianne Feinstein, until she joined newly elected Governor Gray Davis' administration as cabinet secretary (overseeing more than 100 agencies, departments, boards, and commissions) and deputy chief of staff in 1999.

When the energy crisis hit California in mid-2000 and shattered the calm and positive state of affairs Davis experienced in his first eighteen months in office, Kennedy coordinated efforts to fast-track construction of new power plants and promoted energy savings through conservation. Davis was re-elected in November 2002 and the following month appointed Kennedy to the California Public Utilities Commission, where she led the effort to eliminate most of the detailed economic regulation of the telecom industry. She also had a strong interest in enhanced energy efficiency and became the PUC's lead commissioner on the issue.

In October 2003, the voters recalled Gray Davis and elected Arnold Schwarzenegger as governor. A few weeks later, following a meeting between the two, Schwarzenegger and Kennedy began an email correspondence on critical issues facing the state. Their common decisiveness and a no-nonsense approach to decision-making led the Republican governor to appoint Kennedy, a Democrat, to be his chief of staff in 2005.

The reaction in Sacramento by members of both parties ranged from disbelief to outrage. But the partnership clicked. The Schwarzenegger administration had a strong environmental-energy agenda: rooftop solar, cutting through red tape to build thousands of megawatts of renewable plants, enactment of the landmark Assembly Bill 32, the Global Warming Solutions Act, and more. For the environment, these were golden years. The Schwarzenegger energy-environmental record is Kennedy's record, too.

Since 2011, when Schwarzenegger's term ended, Kennedy ran her own consulting company, but her principal effort was the creation of Advanced Microgrid Solutions in 2013, of which she is CEO. By using her technology, a utility can better manage its electrical load, particularly in circumstances such as very hot summer days. Kennedy's company employs some of the newest technologies to enhance energy efficiency and is building the first fleet of hybrid-electric buildings in the world. In recognition of her entrepreneurial spirit, Kennedy has been names one of the 100 Most Creative Business People in the world by the media entity, Fast Company.

S. David Freeman—Energy Adviser to Governor Gray Davis and Lifelong Energy Innovator

© Luis Sinco 2009,
Los Angeles Times

In February 2016, friends held a party to celebrate David Freeman's ninetieth birthday. Freeman danced the night away, showing considerable agility and sway. Guests were given his 2015 book, All-Electric America, *further evidence that he has not slowed down. In 2014, as a consultant on nuclear energy for Friends of the Earth, he spearheaded its efforts to negotiate the closure of the San Onofre Nuclear Generating Station. In 2016, he heralded the upcoming negotiated closure of California's last operating nuclear plant, Diablo Canyon Power Plant, by 2026. Freeman, a long-time critic of nuclear power, has repeatedly articulated his belief that nuclear technology is inherently dangerous.*

A native of Chattanooga, Tennessee, Freeman earned a Bachelor of Science degree from Georgia Tech University and a law degree from the University of Tennessee. After working as a lawyer for the Tennessee Valley Authority, he left to join the Federal Power Commission staff under President John F. Kennedy, and in 1967, President Lyndon Johnson brought Freeman to the White House to coordinate national energy policy. He stayed in the position during the Nixon administration until mid-1971. Next, he went to the Ford Foundation in New York, where he wrote the seminal book, A Time to Choose, *stating the case for making energy conservation and efficiency a national priority. President Jimmy Carter appointed Freeman as chairman of the Tennessee Valley Authority, where he set about making radical changes, stopping construction of its nuclear power plants, reducing the air pollutant sulfur oxide by one-half, and beginning a massive energy conservation program.*

Freeman then headed to the Austin, Texas-based Lower Colorado River Authority. His move to California came in 1990, when he became general manager of the Sacramento Municipal Utility District (SMUD). Dubbed an "eco-pioneer," Freeman oversaw the closing of SMUD's Rancho Seco nuclear power plant facility following a referendum. At

SMUD he emphasized new initiatives in energy efficiency and became a leading advocate of electric vehicles.

He left SMUD to briefly head the New York Power Authority under Governor Mario Cuomo in 1994 and returned to California to help implement the 1996 electricity deregulation law. The next stop for Freeman was Los Angeles, where he worked as deputy mayor of energy and environment for Mayor Antonio Villaraigosa. He then became general manager of the nation's largest municipal utility, the Los Angeles Department of Water and Power. There, he successfully reduced the agency's massive debt, stressed the need to invest in energy efficiency and renewable resources, and led the effort to settle the years-long Owens Valley water dispute.

When the energy crisis hit in 2000, Freeman joined the team of volunteers working in the governor's office to end the brownouts and price spikes caused by the market manipulation of Enron and its allies. As one of a handful of people, as detailed in Chapter Six, he helped break the back of the California energy crisis.

Freeman's hallmarks are an early and lasting interest in energy efficiency and alternative-fueled vehicles and opposition to nuclear power and coal, believing early on that renewable energy must be the emphasis of public policy.

CHAPTER 6

CRISIS BRINGS REFORM

As the immediate impacts of the energy crisis began to fade, attention turned to what came next and what lessons were learned from California's trip down the deregulation road. There was general recognition that the great effort to deregulate electricity had been a resounding failure, although there was little agreement as to why. There were many seats at the banquet of blame: poorly drafted legislation, the lack of true competition in the wholesale market, market manipulation, an unresponsive Federal Energy Regulatory Commission (FERC), low hydro in the Northwest, failed political and regulatory leadership. Whether driven by fear, ideology, or just poor timing, the governor and Public Utilities Commission (PUC) had failed to help the people in a timely manner. Such negative circumstances can create restlessness and new opportunities.

Placing much greater emphasis on conservation as a means of meeting a significant portion of the state's electrical needs had long been the goal of environmental organizations such as the Natural Resources Defense Council (NRDC) and the Environmental Defense Fund (EDF). The energy saving philosophy was enshrined in state law when the California Energy Commission was created in 1974. Still, interest in, and support for, energy conservation waxed and waned for years. It was high when oil prices were high, such as during the first and second Arab oil embargoes of the 1970s. Then interest dropped sharply when oil and natural gas prices dropped.

Again, as part of a multi-pronged program to end the energy crisis, the state legislature in 2001 passed, and Governor Davis signed into law, a bill authorizing California to spend $850 million on programs to reduce electrical demand through conservation.[174] Programs were created to insulate homes of low-income residents, provide rebates for new energy-efficient appliances, give incentives to cut consumption by businesses, and begin major public awareness programs to herald the virtues of energy savings.[175]

The California Consumer Power and Conservation Financing Authority was also created and authorized to issue up to $5 billion in revenue bonds to sponsor and promote energy efficiency, build and own power plants, expand renewables, and update power plants and natural gas transmission.[176] For a variety of reasons, almost none of these goals was achieved. But on October 4, 2001, two Power Authority board members, Donald Vial, a longtime state government official who had been PUC president in the 1980s, and Sunne McPeak, head of the Bay Area Council, a business advocacy group in the San Francisco region, met with the PUC's Michael Peevey in San Francisco to discuss and develop a new energy resource strategy. From this meeting sprang the "loading order," which, in a major and radical step, designated energy efficiency as the number one way to address growing electricity demand.[177] *(See Appendix II)*

Up to this time, when California needed more electricity, it usually built another electric plant. The new loading order policy said, in effect: Before building a new fossil fuel electric plant, first decrease electric demand by increasing energy efficiency and leveling the demand for electricity (such as smoothing out the demand peaks on hot summer afternoons). After lowering electric demand through efficiency and reshaping demand, meet new generation needs with renewable and distributed generation resources. As a last resort, new, clean fossil-fueled plants can be built.

This 2001 draft was prescient in anticipating and addressing the impacts and perils of climate change.

On October 5, 2001, McPeak presented the loading order at a meeting of the Power Authority. This was its public unveiling. In short order, it produced consternation among power plant builders and utility officials, who believed adopting a "save-energy-before-you build-more" path to meeting California's future electrical needs would be perilous, certainly for their industries. Some labor unions, public officials, and engineering, construction, and design firms shared their concerns. They were worried that this upset the old and accepted orderly way of meeting future energy needs and that a "softer path" could lead to higher costs, unreliable electricity, and severely negative economic impacts.

In contrast, the environmental community loved the new loading order. Organizations including the NRDC and the EDF thought it made not only environmental sense but also economic sense and pointed the way toward a better California. Ralph Cavanagh of the NRDC has spent much of his life since then promoting, as a national goal, this approach of energy efficiency first. Others have taken up the idea, but in 2001 this was pretty heady wine and a sharp break from the past.

In addition to the environmental community, support for this new policy thrust came from some legislators and the staffs of state regulatory bodies, such as the PUC and the CEC.

In March 2002, Michael Peevey was appointed as a PUC commissioner, and soon was elevated to president. Peevey and commissioners Geoffrey Brown and Henry Duque began to vote mostly as a bloc, setting in motion bitter disagreements on energy issues with commissioners Lynch and Wood.[178] It seemed every issue of consequence was divisive and usually settled by a 3 to 2 vote.[179] Governor Gray Davis was reelected that November and appointed Susan Kennedy, his cabinet secretary, to the PUC, beginning in January 2003,[180] succeeding Duque, the last Republican commissioner, whose term had ended. Kennedy joined Peevey and Brown in the majority, and the three determined to rehabilitate the PUC after its dismal performance throughout the deregulation crisis and make it a cutting-edge energy policy agency.

The loading order evolved over time and became both broader and more detailed. The document came to articulate a set of policies and practices that would guide state policy for many years. It became officially the Energy Action Plan (EAP) and, in part, reflects lessons learned from the energy crisis.

As one might expect when three powerful state agencies get together to hammer out a plan, it took some work. The final plan required many drafts and redrafts by the staffs at the PUC, CEC, and the Power Authority.[181] Finally, in early 2003, the three agencies produced a single document. It was influenced heavily by the recent catastrophic energy crisis and the future need and desire for cleaner energy. With blackouts and bankruptcy in the rearview mirror, the agency staffs looked ahead to avoiding outages and excessive price increases, as well as more efficient use of energy, while being "sensitive to the implications of energy policy on global climate change and the environment generally."

The three agencies wanted to "send a signal . . . that California is a good place to do business and that investments in the more efficient use of energy and new electricity and natural gas infrastructure will be rewarded."

The energy plan's goals emphasized conservation, building new power generation to ensure affordable and high-quality power, accelerating goals for renewable resource generation, and upgrading and expanding infrastructure to ensure a reliable and reasonably priced supply of natural gas. **(See Appendix III)**

The agencies, which did not always work together or coordinate their efforts smoothly, promised something new and refreshing: cooperation, coordination, the sharing of information and analyses, and the making of joint recommendations to the governor and legislature. They aimed to avert what had happened in the past by developing an "early warning system" to alert policymakers to potential problems and by working with the FERC to redesign market rules and prevent potential manipulation of the energy markets. "[182]

Two of the plan's goals have seen much progress to date: To "partner with governmental and other groups in western North America to pursue commonly held energy standards" and to work "to minimize the energy industry's impact on climate change."

The bold and far-reaching policies of the EAP were controversial. Largely because its concepts seemed so forward-thinking and almost radical, much of business was opposed, as was nearly all of the energy industry, with the exception of companies supporting greater use of renewable energy, such as wind and solar. There were those who believed it represented too intrusive a government. Further, the EAP was technology-promoting and -inducing. Some of the cautious state bureaucracy also was opposed, fearing this was too big a step for California and its own agencies to carry out.

On April 18, 2003, the plan was adopted by a unanimous vote of the Power Authority governing board.[183] On April 30, 2003, it was adopted by unanimous vote by the CEC.[184] On May 8, the PUC adopted it by a vote of 3 to 2, with commissioners Lynch and Wood dissenting.[185]

Throughout the balance of the decade, the energy agencies met collectively in public session three to four times a year to review events and set in motion new joint actions. Though the composition of the governing board changed over time and the Power Authority ceased to function eighteen months later, the central thrust of the EAP, which occasionally is amended and updated, has not changed. In fact, one of the great accomplishments of the energy plan was the various energy agencies working together and the sense of cooperation it bred, which was a welcome departure from the bureaucratic infighting and refusal to cooperate that had dogged the agencies in prior years.

The election of Jerry Brown in 2010 as governor for the third time, after a hiatus of twenty-eight years, brought a new mechanism for policy cooperation and coordination, which continues since his reelection in 2014. The Brown administration convenes the energy principals regularly. It invites the chairs and presidents of the energy and environmental agencies, along with members of the governor's staff and assorted others, to meet with Brown often. Still today, new energy policy ideas are often conceived in this forum.

The Energy Action Plan in its first iteration strongly supported aggressive targets for renewable energy as part of California's resource mix. But the state's renewables commitment extended back years earlier. In the 1980s, as noted in Chapter Three, Edison and Luz cooperated in building more than 350 megawatts of parabolic trough solar technology in the Mojave Desert. Geothermal development in the Imperial Valley and in northern San Bernardino County at the Coso Geothermal Field grew rapidly, as did wind energy—aided by generous federal tax credits—in the Palm Springs area in northern Los Angeles County, and the Altamont Pass in the Bay Area's Alameda County.[186] [187] Biomass and small hydroelectric facilities also were developed, though on a lesser scale.[188]

In 2002, the legislature passed, and Governor Davis signed into law, Senate Bill 1078, which established the Renewables Portfolio Standard (RPS) program.[189] The legislation, which had bipartisan support, required that 20 percent of the electrical sales of the investor-owned utilities come from renewable energy by 2017.[190] This was trumped by the original EAP, which accelerated the 20 percent requirement to 2010. While the plan was not a statutory require-ment—that is, not a law—this action made it clear that the energy policymakers in the state would do all in their power to speed up the adoption of renewables. And, as is often the case, the legisla-ture followed agency lead, passing Senate Bill 107 in 2006.[191] This bill, signed by Governor Schwarzenegger, embedded into law the mandate that 20 percent of the state's electricity be generated by renewables by 2010.[192] The bill also made clear that the 20 percent target applied to both private and municipal utilities.

The game of hopscotch continued. The EAP was revised in 2005 as EAP II; it stated a new goal: California utilities must generate 33 per-cent of their electricity from renewables by 2020. That goal was then established in a 2008 executive order by Governor Schwarzenegger, long a champion of renewable energy, particularly solar. The follow-ing year, he issued an executive order directing the Air Resources Board, exercising its authority under Assembly Bill 32, to adopt regu-lations to help insure the 33 percent goal would be met.

Two years later, Governor Brown signed into law Senate Bill X1-2, which codified 33 percent renewables by 2020 and made clear that the law included the investor-owned utilities regulated by the PUC, as well as municipal utilities, independent energy providers, and com-munity choice aggregators.[193] (As mentioned, Brown has subsequently indicated that renewables should represent 50 percent of all electric generation by 2030. The California legislature is talking about a po-tential goal of 100 percent renewables by 2050.) While all the ex-ecutive branch actions and statutory enactments had opposition from various business interests, and to some extent both private and pub-lic utilities, very little outright hostility was displayed. The leaders of the state—politicians and government officials, businesses, environ-mental and other nonprofit organizations, and the professions—have come to accept the energy path California has chosen. In the words of Governor Brown, upon signing Senate Bill X1-2:

"This bill will bring many important benefits to California, includ-ing stimulating investment in green technologies in the state, creating tens of thousands of new jobs, improving local air quality, promoting energy independence, and reducing greenhouse gas emissions."[194]

Of course, of all the renewable technologies, solar, in all its forms, seemed the most glamorous and particularly well suited for sunny California. And it had an active champion—Arnold Schwarzenegger.

**IVANPAH SOLAR THERMAL POWER PLANT, LOCATED
IN CALIFORNIA'S MOJAVE DESERT.**

Courtesy of BrightSource Energy

CHAPTER 7

"CONSIDER THAT A DIVORCE"
— *Arnold Schwarzenegger, after shooting Sharon Stone in* **Total Recall**

In 2003, Californians divorced Governor Davis through a recall election, in large part over the energy crisis, and simultaneously elected as governor Arnold Schwarzenegger, a man with no governing experience. There was plenty of competition: 135 candidates were on the ballot, from political commentator Arianna Huffington and porn hustler Larry Flynt to former baseball commissioner Peter Ueberroth and Lieutenant Governor Cruz Bustamante. But the Austrian-born movie star with a heavy accent, who announced his intention to run for governor on Jay Leno's late night television show, was the victor on October 7, 2003.

Schwarzenegger presided over the state in a time of great change and economic challenge, while developing and implementing a bipartisan approach to energy policy and air quality issues. And he broke dramatic new ground in his determination to adopt policies and programs to mitigate climate change.

Shortly after his election, Schwarzenegger invited Public Utilities Commission (PUC) President Michael Peevey and Commissioner Susan Kennedy to Sacramento. Schwarzenegger usually received people in a tent (where he could smoke cigars) on the grass inside the courtyard of the gubernatorial offices. After the first order of business—a photo for the visitors with the movie star/new governor—was completed, Schwarzenegger demanded a briefing on energy issues. He was keenly conscious of what had brought his predecessor to the ignominious end of his political career and was determined to become expert on the energy issue.

The conversation ranged over many topics, but climate change and solar energy seemed to be the governor's special interest. Schwarzenegger spoke about his good friend, James Cameron, who directed him in the *Terminator* series and also directed *Titanic* and *Avatar*. Cameron apparently had difficulty arranging for installation of a rooftop solar array atop his Los Angeles home. Schwarzenegger asked whether the PUC could help Cameron and, at the same time, expressed his support for a major effort to expand solar energy throughout the state.

The meeting was consequential in at least two respects. First, it introduced the governor to Democrat Susan Kennedy, who eventually left the PUC and became Schwarzenegger's chief of staff. Second, the governor showed his early advocacy for solar.

Not long afterward, Schwarzenegger announced his support for legislation by Democratic Senator Kevin Murray of Los Angeles, co-authored by Republican Assemblyman (and later Congressman) John Campbell of Orange County, to enact the governor's "Million Solar Roofs" initiative into law.[195] The measure would have required home-builders of projects with more than fifty homes to offer solar panels to homebuyers. There was general support for the legislation, but it foundered over the insistence of a Democrat-controlled Assembly committee that installers of solar systems on commercial facilities be paid prevailing union wages.[196] The Republican governor and Campbell balked at such a provision because of the expense it would add to the project; they withdrew their support, and the legislation was not passed in 2005.[197] The same fate prevailed in 2006.

Schwarzenegger, visibly frustrated by the legislature's inaction and the inability to work out a compromise on the labor issues, did what most governors would do in a similar situation. He called upon his own administration to get what he wanted done through an arm of the executive branch, the PUC. He asked Peevey if the PUC on its own, without legislation, could create a program that would put solar panels on a million rooftops. Peevey told the governor the answer was yes, that legally, the PUC could create such a program, though some aspects, such as the then-emerging interest in what has come to be known as Net Energy Metering (NEM) would require legislation.[198] Pleased, the governor soon thereafter issued an executive order to the PUC, and it began developing what became known as the California Solar Initiative (CSI).[199]

Working together, the PUC and the California Energy Commission issued a joint report in June 2005 that analyzed the critical issues surrounding the creation of the solar initiative.[200] The PUC at the same time opened a proceeding to get input from the multitude of parties interested in the development of a new solar program.[201] Prior to this, the state had only a few small solar programs. These efforts, though of value, were haphazard and continually ran out of money.

In January 2006, the PUC voted 3 to 1 to establish the California Solar Initiative. The previous month, the PUC had voted to provide $300 million for incentives for solar projects.[202] Now this decision went much further. It was big, committing to provide $2.9 billion of incentives for solar development over eleven years.[203] This was going to be a Schwarzenegger legacy.

Never before had the state thrown its weight behind such an ambitious energy effort—to develop 3,000 megawatts of solar energy by the end of 2016.[204] The regulatory action mirrored the goal of the state legislature's Senate Bill 1, the governor's "Million Solar Roofs" proposal, which had failed to pass. So instead of resulting from a law, the CSI began as a regulatory program articulating the desire to make California a world leader in solar power.

As often happens, the legislature was now in the position of playing catch-up. Eight months after the PUC had acted, the legislature, in August 2006, finally passed Senate Bill 1, and the governor signed it into law.[205] The balance of the year saw the PUC integrating into its adopted solar initiative the language and impacts of the legislative action.[206] The revised program was launched on New Year's Day, 2007.

The solar initiative's budget and megawatt goal were both revised downward in the face of the dollars available. In the end, the cost was not quite $2.367 billion over ten years, with the revised goal of reaching 1,940 megawatts of installed solar capacity by the end of 2016, of which 190 megawatts would be for low-income programs[207] (SASH—Single Family Affordable Solar Homes—and MASH—Multifamily Affordable Solar Homes).[208]

Soon, Senate Bill 1's co-author, Kevin Murray, included other extensive features in his bill, such as the Energy Commission's program to promote solar on new homes and a requirement that municipal utilities, such as the Los Angeles Department of Water and Power and the Sacramento Municipal Utility District, among others, offer their customers solar energy. Including the municipal utilities in the effort, dubbed Go Solar California, brought the target back to 3,000 megawatts of solar by the end of 2016, at an estimated cost of more than $3.5 billion.[209]

The program, by most all judgments, has been an unqualified success. Perhaps the most notable feature of the solar initiative was its novel incentive-level design. In this, the designers decided not to follow the prevailing European solar rate structure, the Feed-In Tariff, which pays a rooftop solar customer directly for feeding renewable power into the grid, whether or not the utility can use the power. This gives hefty and continuing subsidies to solar energy.[210] Instead, the California solar program was committed to making solar energy subsidy-free and standing on its own economically by the end of the program. It succeeded. In the words of Lyndon Rive, CEO of SolarCity, the nation's largest rooftop installer, "California's contribution to a renewable world was to make the solar industry self-supporting, without subsidies."

The CSI goal was to quickly grow the industry and to see product improvements and declining prices. But how? The PUC staff, helped by a variety of economists, energy planners, engineers, and public policy consultants devised a declining block-incentive program, announced in January 2006.[211] They divided the overall megawatt goal into ten incentive-level steps, starting at $2.80 per watt,[212] reducing incrementally an average of 10 percent per step. Once certain megawatt targets were reached, the incentive would decline and, at the end of ten years, it would end.

This was established to happen automatically. Once a certain megawatt level was reached, beginning in 50 megawatt increments and growing larger each year, down came the subsidy, from $2.80 a watt in 2006 to $.25 a watt in 2016.[213] But the program proved so successful that all subsidy levels were used up in eight years, not the ten years originally envisioned.[214] As of this writing, the California Solar Initiative has met all its goals, faster and at lower cost than its architects expected, helped immeasurably by the sharp drop in the cost of rooftop solar panels due to competitive Chinese manufacturers.

There are several reasons for this success: 1) The ten-step incentive approach was created and never changed, providing regulatory certainty—a vital component often missing in government; this certainty in some ways is a bedrock of California's successful air quality and energy programs, extending far beyond solar. 2) Certainty overcame one of the most anticipated concerns of the program—that sales would drop as the subsidy declined—but they actually increased as public support for solar grew. 3) The PUC adopted and enforced strong consumer protections to ensure that a few bad actors would not tarnish the program. 4) Transparency was achieved as the PUC made available the data on sales, including the names of manufacturers and installers. This increased confidence in the program by commercial interests and various competitive firms.[215]

The research-focused Solar Development Program was also deemed a success. Its expenditure of $50 million spurred new demonstrations and improvements in the technology and, equally important, indisputably helped make California the nation's solar center as it drew more research dollars to the state and its national laboratories and other research institutions.[216] The private-sector company Itron managed this program. Around the same time, AB 32, the California Global Warming Solutions Act of 2006, was passed by the legislature. Governor Schwarzenegger, in a bipartisan partnership with State Assembly Speaker Fabian Nunez, assured the bill became law. Perhaps the signature achievement of the Schwarzenegger administration it remains the most far-reaching climate change legislation enacted in the nation.

So it was no wonder that Governor Arnold Schwarzenegger was grinning in April 2007 as he looked at *Newsweek* magazine. There he was, on the cover, spinning a globe like a basketball on his index finger, with the headline, "Save the Planet or Else."[217] It was actually a very well-deserved accolade. After his shakedown cruise establishing leadership in solar, he looked to even bigger accomplishments. He inscribed his name on AB 32 in a ceremony so orchestrated that it brought in Tony Blair, the prime minister of Great Britain, live via satellite onto an enormous screen alongside the governor.

This bill-signing ceremony was not held in Schwarzenegger's office or on the Capitol steps but was an elaborate, invitation-only moment set up by Hollywood events specialists. It was staged on Treasure Island, a man-made island and former naval base in the San Francisco Bay between San Francisco and Oakland. With a view of the Pacific Ocean stretching out toward China and beyond, and the orange Golden Gate Bridge in the distance, Schwarzenegger wanted everyone to understand the worldwide importance of California's new leadership on climate change. A similar ceremony took place the following day in Southern California.

**GOVERNOR SCHWARZENEGGER SIGNS AB 32, THE
CALIFORNIA GLOBAL WARMING SOLUTIONS ACT, IN
THE MIDDLE OF SAN FRANCISCO BAY, 2006.**
Courtesy of Getty Images

Schwarzenegger really did deserve credit for more than his signature and a flashy ceremony. First of all, the law itself was not glitzy and Hollywood-like. It is a stringent, overarching requirement for California to substantially reduce its greenhouse gas emissions in every sector of the economy.[218] It requires California to reduce such emissions to 1990 levels by 2020—an approximately 15 percent reduction below emissions growth absent any regulation.[219] Even better, the ARB, the PUC, and the CEC had a pretty good sense of how to get there.

The law requires improved energy efficiency above already rigorous energy efficiency standards for buildings and appliances, expanded renewable energy use, cleaner transportation, and waste reduction.[220] The law reflects the apex of the solutions California has been pursuing for years, only more difficult, more sophisticated, and more intrusive. It is the approach every country on the globe will have to establish if the world is really going to reduce greenhouse gas emissions.

As always, California styled its tough regulations, not as expensive and detrimental to the California lifestyle, but as another way to insure a strong economy, provide better public health, and protect the air, the sea, the mountains, and the deserts. In the words of Mary Nichols, chair of the ARB, the agency charged with enforcing AB 32, "There is no doubt that we need this law, or any question that we will put it into practice with rigor across the entire economy." Nichols was the perfect person to implement this law fairly, legally, and with patience, technical excellence, and consistency, in keeping with her reputation and skill set. She would build a legal framework and drape the final greenhouse gas reduction requirements over strong, unassailable regulatory scaffolding.

In his own way, Schwarzenegger's actions reflected a similar approach. He didn't just sign a bill that had floated across his desk. He started California down the official path to the law in 2004, signing a series of executive orders that provided the basis for AB 32.[221] An executive order, whether signed by a governor or president of the United States, has the same force as a law—but only while that chief executive is in office. Some executive orders are never meant or able to really change things. For example, Schwarzenegger's executive order on building a hydrogen highway in California never came to fruition.[222]

In California, on many important environmental issues, the executive order is often seen as the first draft of a law the legislature will someday codify for a life after the governor who signs it has moved on. Schwarzenegger signed several such key orders and ancillary bills that provided teeth for AB 32. They addressed reduced energy use, requesting a waiver from the federal EPA to secure the ability for California to regulate greenhouse gases from passenger vehicles, establishing a Low Carbon Fuel Standard and the Million Solar Roof Initiative, regulating sprawl, and increasing California's Renewable Portfolio Standard.[223]

The important environmental executive orders are often short and seem general in scope. But don't be fooled; they are well researched by environmental, business, and agency technocrats to be stretch but doable targets and tasks. Initial coalitions of support are assembled. Often, these early coalitions are not big or powerful enough to get a law passed, but they are solid enough so that a governor who wants to provide leadership has the political strength and clout to sign an executive order.

Schwarzenegger, the Hummer-loving Republican who built up a personal fortune from smart business acumen investing his acting revenues, decided early on that he wanted to make a political name for himself, not only as an environmentalist but as a specific type of environmentalist—a global environmentalist.[224]

At different times, Schwarzenegger attributed his environmental leanings to various roots. Sometimes he would say that growing up in Austria cultivated an undying love of green mountains and sparkling streams.[225] Other times he said that he often had respiratory problems in his early weightlifting days on Muscle Beach in Venice, California, due to lousy air quality.[226] On other occasions, he started a conversation with, "My friend, James Cameron, says," and a strongly worded comment on solar energy, electric cars, or lowering energy use would emerge.

James Cameron and Gale Anne Hurd are the two Hollywood producers who helped make Arnold Schwarzenegger's career. Although he had a charming accent, a clever tongue, and a physique worth a nice bit of income, playing Conan the Barbarian didn't exactly put Arnold on the Hollywood "A" list. But then one day, Cameron and Hurd took the future governor to lunch at The Polo Lounge and asked him to star in their new movie, *The Terminator*. Two of the lifetime outcomes from that lunch were Arnold's signature phrase, "I'll be back!" and James Cameron's friendship. Cameron, well known for writing and directing all the *Terminator* movies, *Aliens, Titanic, Avatar,* and many others, is almost as famous as an avid environmentalist, with a strong and lasting influence on Arnold Schwarzenegger.

In fact, the impact of filmmaking, one of California's top local industries, is too deeply discounted overall as a key to California's long-term success story on the environment. Cameron's hit film *Avatar* was released in 2009, when the United States was filled with climate change doubters. The opening lines of Cameron's script set up the reality:

"The Earth is dying ... covered with a gray mold of human civilization. ... Overpopulation, overdevelopment, nuclear terrorism, environmental warfare tactics, radiation leakage from power plants and waste dumps, toxic waste, air pollution, deforestation, pollution, and overfishing of the oceans, global warming, ozone depletion, loss of biodiversity through extinction ... all of these have combined to make the once green and beautiful a terminal cesspool."

Three years before *Avatar*, Al Gore's *An Inconvenient Truth* made believers out of many, while at the same time, *Happy Feet*, about penguins losing the ice environment they need in order to live, was setting up the next generation of environmentalists and educating their parents, too, about global warming.

About a half a million Californians work in the film industry, one of the biggest job creators in the state. Even Governor Brown—who is more likely to be reading a tome on environmental economics on a Saturday night than taking in *The Day After Tomorrow*, a thriller in which climate change forces Californians to illegally emigrate to the warmer clime of Mexico—is heavily influenced by Hollywood. The producers and actors who pop into his office and receptions have both deep pockets and strong opinions.

Profile in Leadership
Terry Tamminen—Secretary, Environmental Protection Agency

© Rick Meyer 2011,
Los Angeles Times

In, on, or about the water sums up a good portion of environmental leader Terry Tamminen. Now living in Santa Monica, Tamminen, born in Wisconsin, lived in Texas and Mexico before his family moved to Los Angeles. Enchanted by the ocean, he received scuba lessons for his twelfth birthday and shortly afterward was diving off the rocky Palos Verdes Peninsula cliffs. Later, he was off to Brisbane, Australia, where his father had a tropical fish-breeding business, and then he traveled through Europe.

He graduated from California State University, Northridge in 1975 with a degree in theater arts, but he hit the road again, eventually managing the largest sheep ranch east of the Mississippi while working with the University of Minnesota on controlling disease in livestock. He later went into the swimming pool-cleaning business in Malibu and Beverly Hills, catering to a celebrity clientele. He sold his company and wrote a guide to pool maintenance now in its third edition.

He eventually turned his attention to environmental issues, launching the nonprofit Santa Monica Baykeeper, a preservation group that is part of a network of Waterkeeper groups he co-founded to protect the nation's waterways. He became acquainted with national environmental activist Robert Kennedy, son of the late senator and related by marriage to Arnold Schwarzenegger, whose then-wife, Maria Shriver, was a Kennedy.

In 2003, Tamminen and longtime Schwarzenegger friend and confidante Bonnie Reiss worked long hours as the future governor's campaign advisers on environmental policy. Upon his election, Schwarzenegger named Tamminen secretary of the California Environmental Protection Agency. Tamminen was the large caliber weapon Schwarzenegger used to accomplish air, solar and ocean programs. His environmental agenda was broad: regulating CO_2 emissions, replacing—with incentives—older polluting diesel engines, and activating the program to build a California Hydrogen Highway Network of 200 fueling stations. He also advocated for solar roofs and opened freeway carpool lanes to hybrid vehicles, a popular program that stimulated electric- and hybrid-vehicle sales.

Based on these accomplishments, the governor asked Tamminen to become his cabinet secretary. Today, Tamminen is the CEO of the Leonardo DiCaprio Foundation and author of several books about climate and environmental issues, including Lives Per Gallon: The True Cost of Our Oil Addiction, Cracking the Carbon Code, and Watercolors: How JJ the Whale Saved Us. He is currently editing a three-volume work on Shakespeare.

CHAPTER 8

DRIVE CALIFORNIA

The push to improve California's poor air quality through energy efficiency and more renewable power, alongside the desire to reduce the negative impacts of human-caused climate change, continued throughout Arnold Schwarzenegger's seven years as governor. At times there were pitched battles, not only in Sacramento, but also in Washington, D.C. Outcomes were often in doubt for months and years on end.

Implementing AB 32, the Global Warming Solutions Act of 2006, is justly celebrated as the heart of California's twenty-first century environmental leadership. It addresses energy, transportation, and all things that touch them along radical new paths that have so far been successful.

Having the ability to regulate greenhouse gas emissions from cars and light trucks became a keystone of California managing and leading the way on reducing emissions. Cleaning up energy had been within the state's purview, and it had acted early, often, and with great originality to reduce greenhouse gas emissions. But each successful reduction in stationary emissions meant transportation became a larger percentage of the sources of greenhouse gas emissions left to reduce.

Because of the importance of its transportation impacts, AB 32 would have been of much less consequence if Schwarzenegger had failed to get a federal waiver to allow California to dictate automotive greenhouse gas emissions under a previous California law, AB 1493, signed by Governor Davis in July 2002. That law took the seminal approach of classifying greenhouse gas as a pollutant and, over time, normalizing and legalizing that concept.[227] Legalizing it took a while, though. The US Environmental Protection Agency (EPA) didn't give California the federal waiver needed to implement AB 1493 until 2009, after Barack Obama became president.[228]

For many years, California had the right and the inclination, and took the action, to regulate emissions from stationary sources such as refineries and power plants—anything with a smokestack. But regulation of cars and trucks was largely the jurisdiction of the federal government, unless the national government granted a waiver to allow a state to regulate independently.

Without a waiver granted to California, tailpipe emission controls were solely a federal prerogative. Both the federal government and the automakers were like dragons ferociously guarding this "federal only" jurisdiction. The automakers knew that having stricter regulations imposed by California—their biggest market—would inevitably lead to them having to make changes in all cars sold nationally.

Tailpipe emissions were not really directly regulated at all, even by the feds. The only control of tailpipe emission was through national automotive fuel economy standards set by the National Highway Traffic Safety Administration.[229] The agency had last set new standards in 1975 and saw no pressing need to update them, pretty much ever.[230]

By 2002, stationery-stack emissions had been reduced enough in California that cars and trucks constituted an ever-larger percentage of the state's underlying air quality problem. State Assemblywoman Fran Pavley and her environmental cohorts believed it was time to regulate tailpipe emissions. They approached the problem through a flanking maneuver.

Pavley introduced AB 1493—the groundbreaking and brilliant legislation that gave California the authority to achieve "the maximum feasible reduction" of greenhouse gases emitted by passenger vehicles and light-duty trucks.[231] The primary greenhouse gas coming from tailpipes was CO_2.[232] When AB 1493 was signed by Governor Davis in 2002, California was going to be the first jurisdiction in the world to regulate greenhouse gases from tailpipes.[233]

As noted earlier, Schwarzenegger addressed climate change in a serious and long-term manner. He accomplished many things, but perhaps one of the most important, and most unsung, was to wrest the needed California waiver from the hands of the federal government.

Overriding federal jurisdiction like this would not be easy. California's reasoning was artful, cunning, and untested. It had two key parts: First, it had to get CO_2 recognized as a pollutant, and then the state needed to get its typical waiver under the federal Clean Air Act in order to regulate it.

The biggest leap forward in the new law was that it announced and assumed that CO_2 was a pollutant because it caused global warming. Hardly anyone in either the scientific or policy communities really thought of CO_2 as a classic pollutant in 2002. After all, humans "emit" CO_2 every time they breathe. How could you regulate breathing? If you created and expelled CO_2 in your own body, it was clearly not a toxic threat to health. There was much joking throughout the nation that year, along the order of "California is so kooky it is going to make everyone hold his breath to address global warming."

But California's leap was to say that if CO_2 caused global warming, it was *prima facie* a pollutant. Therefore, it could be regulated under Section 177, California's exemption allowing it to regulate pollutants under the Clean Air Act. By 2005, the California ARB had done in-depth research to make its case that greenhouse gases were pollutants. The state applied to the federal EPA for a Clean Air Act waiver to regulate greenhouse gases at the state level.

President George W. Bush's EPA declined to respond formally, on the grounds that the Clean Air Act did not have a mandate for a federal standard for greenhouse gas emissions, and therefore, the agency did not have the authority to give California a waiver for something that wasn't covered under the Clean Air Act.[234] The clear message was that California shouldn't bother applying. Eleven states, fourteen environmental groups and two cities immediately sued the EPA for assuming such a narrow interpretation of the law.[235]

California knew that in passing AB 1493, it was taking the long view. The state did not expect to start actually controlling greenhouse gas emissions in the short term. In fact, it took seven years from passing the bill to receiving the federal waiver. The first requirement for auto fleet greenhouse gas adjustments wasn't promulgated until 2004 by the ARB, and it required about a 22 percent greenhouse gas reduction in 2009 car models.[236] The ARB's report underlying the regulation was highly technical, evidence-based, painstaking, and complete.

The report laid out the basic legal defense that would be used by California to justify greenhouse gases being classed as pollutants. An in-depth analysis detailed how a 22 percent reduction by 2009, as well as subsequent further reductions, were achievable. It had the intellectual honesty to announce that these requirements would initially add more than $300 to the price of a new car in California. That would be partially offset by lower operating costs, but, over time, cars would cost consumers even more.

California approached this radical idea of classifying greenhouse gases as pollutants with consistency and courage. When the ARB announced that greenhouse gas controls would be expensive, it also concluded, with evidence, that there were net positive benefits for Californians' health and well-being and the state's economy. The public stood by this argument and continued to support and elect officials who would implement these policies. And though politicians and appointees would come and go, the technically proficient state bureaucrats, especially at the ARB, were heavily invested in science and prepared for a long fight to win. In this battle, the research talent at California's public and private universities aided tremendously.

Those opposed—the federal government, automakers, and oil companies—were also entrenched and clearly saw this interpretation of greenhouse gases as a pollutant as a do-or-die turning point. There were many court cases challenging the California law and those of other states that adopted the same "clean cars" legislation as California.[237] The legal battles have been chronicled often, especially the automakers' decision to feint. They did not directly challenge the behemoth California in the courts, but instead sued what they viewed as "ninety-pound weaklings" within the group of states that had also adopted the California rule. Vermont and Massachusetts were the defendants in an automaker suit to prove that greenhouse gases were not pollutants.[238]

In 2007, the US Supreme Court declared in favor of Massachusetts that CO2 could be considered a pollutant.[239] This meant that California had successfully overcome a major hurdle to implement Assembly Bill 1493. Now that greenhouse gases had been declared a pollutant under the Clean Air Act, California just needed to get its federal waiver to regulate these emissions in vehicles, and a brave new world would open up.

California applied for its federal waiver to regulate greenhouse gases from tailpipes immediately after the Massachusetts victory.[240] It was the

73rd waiver for which the state had applied under the Clean Air Act, and the first seventy-two had been granted. However, this was 2007, and Bush—more an ally of the opponents than of the state of California— was president. EPA Administrator Stephen Johnson did not grant the waiver, ignoring the recommendations of senior staff, including one EPA official who told Johnson the credibility of the agency "will be irreparably damaged" if he rejected the waiver request.[241] [242]California was again in limbo in trying to enforce AB 1493.

Governor Schwarzenegger was furious. He held a press conference on the steps of the Capitol and announced he would sue the EPA.[243] He stood with Attorney General Jerry Brown at his side, along with Mary Nichols, his recently appointed head of the ARB. He made headlines across the world. Then he took Nichols and Brown, along with Fran Pavley, the author of AB 1493 and now a state senator, to Washington in his private jet to announce his plans in person. He thundered into the EPA. When Johnson escorted them into his office, Pavley, who always characterizes herself as "just a simple middle school teacher," didn't even recognize him. But Schwarzenegger did. And he became very animated. That did not help.

On February 29, 2008, for the first time ever, the EPA's Johnson issued a regulatory notice formally denying California a Clean Air Act waiver,[244] an action that affected eighteen other states that wanted to adopt California's stricter tailpipe emission standards. It had been three years since California first made its waiver request.

Saying that this stuck in Schwarzenegger's craw was an understatement. He chafed, he complained, he called, he wrote letters and emails, he sent emissaries, he wrote editorial commentaries. He never let up on the issue until the national political scene took another turn. President Bush left office, and Barack Obama, who had criticized the EPA's waiver denial, became president in January 2009. Before the end of the month, the new president wrote a memo to the EPA asking it to reconsider California's waiver denial.[245] In June 2009, EPA Administrator Lisa P. Jackson granted the waiver, three and a half years after the state requested it.[246] Schwarzenegger did a victory dance and dropped for a self-congratulatory push-up.

California hasn't put all its greenhouse gas reduction approaches into one basket. The overarching goal is energy efficiency on every front. Big categories are advanced clean cars, the low carbon fuel standard, and the renewable portfolio standard. Nearly 70 percent of Californians support the stretch goals of the global warming acts passed by the legislature and signed by governors Schwarzenegger and Brown.[247] The goal is to achieve this with both regulatory certainty and positive economic impact to the state. This forward thinking helps account for the fact that California receives $800 million of the global $2 billion in green technology venture capital.[248] Job creation numbers in high tech increase continually. California has about 1.5 million jobs in the energy efficiency sector. New tech job estimates range from 50,000 to 125,000.

One of California's hallmarks in all its climate change actions involves steady, constant progress. Like most successful long-term wars, the state fought its battles on many fronts at once. After awhile, big setbacks became more difficult. The myriad interlocking policies, practices, laws, and regulations became as impenetrable as the thorny wood surrounding Sleeping Beauty in the fairy tale. After a certain point, the thicket is so thick and overlapping that very little long-term damage can be done by any particular enemy.

At least, that was the working theory before President Trump was elected in 2016. Rather than attack any of the interlocking policies and practices mentioned above, his administration proposed chopping down the whole thicket of California exceptionalism on automotive tailpipe regulation by withdrawing the 2009 federal waiver altogether. The underlying reasoning by the Trump EPA for is that California has tightened its requirements for future emissions since 2009, so the waiver is no longer valid. If the government goes ahead on this withdrawal, a long court battle will follow. If California loses its legal standing under the waiver, it may well be forced to give up much of its leadership on auto emission standards.

Governor Brown has gone on the offensive. He has chosen climate action as part of his legacy. Rather than worry about a waiver withdrawal, he has upped the ante and is assuming the mantle of US leadership on greenhouse gas reductions that President Trump has shrugged off. And it's not just a PR dream. California has the experience, the plan, and the will to step-up.

Profile in Leadership
Fran Pavley— Legislative Environmental Leader

Courtesy of
Meeno Peluce

Fran Pavley, a California native, was a middle school teacher for twenty-eight years. She started her political life by being elected the first mayor of Agoura Hills, in Los Angeles County, motivated by her work to curb suburban sprawl in the 1970s and 1980s. Her love of nature, and her desire to preserve it, is obvious at her home. There are drought-tolerant plants instead of a lawn, a clothesline rather than a dryer, no dishwasher, and trees have been planted to shade the house because it has no air conditioning. She has a master's degree in environmental planning from California State University, Northridge.

Pavley may have inherited her political instincts from her great-grandfather, three-time Democratic presidential candidate William Jennings Bryan. Known for his soaring rhetoric in his famous "Cross of Gold" speech when he first ran for the presidency, he also is remembered for his clashes with Clarence Darrow in the famed Scopes trial in Tennessee in 1925.

After serving as various local government chairs in the 1990s, as well as on the California Coastal Commission, Pavley was elected to the state Assembly in 2000. On the statewide stage, she sponsored and promoted a host of environmental and energy issues. In 2002, she carried legislation to reduce vehicle greenhouse gas emissions, a previously unexplored regulatory approach. In a host of important bills over the years, this was perhaps her most significant: Assembly Bill 1493, "the Pavley bill."

Her Assembly Bill 32, introduced in 2006, also was unprecedented, setting the nation's first cap on greenhouse gases. Legislative passage of the bill was very difficult, and it was a cliffhanger. Assembly Speaker Fabian Núñez stepped in and became the bill's lead author, bringing with him forty Assembly Democrats. The bill, signed by Governor Schwarzenegger, garnered California worldwide recognition for its energy and environmental leadership.

To many, AB 32 is the pinnacle of state leadership in acting to reduce greenhouse gases while simultaneously spurring innovation and job growth in clean technology, alternative fuels, renewable energy, and energy efficiency. It is, simply, the foundation upon which California has continued to build its energy-environmental record and serves as a beacon to many people distant from the state.

Two years after the law passed, Pavley was elected to the state Senate, where she continued her active environmental leadership on issues including fracking and groundwater, while also carrying legislation to enhance the state's lagging teacher-training programs and leading legislative efforts to strengthen laws on domestic violence and sexual assault.

In 2015, Pavley wrote Senate Bill 32, which passed both houses of the legislature and was signed by Governor Brown in August 2016. It updates the earlier AB 32, which calls for California reaching 1990 levels of greenhouse gas emissions by 2020. Senate Bill 32 calls for targets 40 percent below 1990 levels by 2030.

Pavley left office at the end of 2016, a departure required by the term limit provisions of California law.

CHAPTER 9

ON THE ENERGY FRONT – STEADY PROGRESS

While continuous achievements were occurring in the air quality field, parallel progress was happening in the energy arena. The state doubled down on its commitment to renewable energy, from windmills and biomass to all forms of solar energy, from central-station generation to rooftop collectors. At the same time, it acted to restrict and ultimately end the use of coal to generate power. The year 2006 also saw many other milestones.

After the Public Utilities Commission (PUC) had implemented the California Solar Initiative, and the California Energy Commission (CEC) was working on setting very high but achievable energy efficiency standards for televisions and, seemingly, everything else that plugged in, the PUC turned to a fundamental tool necessary for the success of solar in California—Net Energy Metering (NEM). In concept, NEM is uncomplicated. It allows any residential or commercial generators of solar power to earn financial credits on their utility bills for power that is generated and fed back to the utility from their own solar panels.[249] The customer is, in effect, a mini power plant. The credit offsets the customer's electricity bill. In other words, all extra electricity generated by a rooftop solar unit goes to the utility to replace dirtier power in the system, and the solar customer gets credit on his or her bill for the power.[250]

This happens monthly, as the bill credits for the excess generation are applied to the customer's bill at the same retail rate that the customer would have paid without the solar system. Given that utility-customer rate structures are tiered—that is, the more you use, the higher the rate paid—"shaving" the top tier is very beneficial to the customer. Also, annually, at the end of a twelve-month billing period, any surplus electricity that has been returned to the utility is trued-up at a rate set by the PUC. So, the consumer who installs a distribution generator (DG) system such as solar gets a monthly bill credit and an annual true-up of his or her bill. Customers who install small-scale wind, biogas, and fuel cell generation are also eligible for the energy metering, though most of the attention and monies are going for solar systems.

This type of metering has made solar very popular, with more than 90 percent of the state's solar systems connected to the utility grid.[251] As of mid-2016, the total number of residential and commercial accounts enrolled in the state's NEM program neared 500,000, with thousands more applications pending.[252]

The legislature, building on the work of the PUC, has scrambled to keep pace with solar's popularity. In 2012, it passed, and Governor Brown signed, SB 594, which allows NEM aggregation. [253] This permits a customer to aggregate the load from multiple meters; the energy metering credits then are shared.[254]

A few years earlier, Governor Schwarzenegger signed Assembly Bill 920, which required the utilities to pay customers annually for the excess electricity produced but not used on-site.[255] Also, a program of the PUC called Virtual Net Metering allows an owner of multi-family housing to allocate the system benefits to tenants in the units.[256] This helps low-income households participate in, and benefit from, solar energy.

All the pro-solar activity at the PUC and the CEC and in the legislature did not happen in a vacuum. The utilities, to varying degrees, were opposed to net metering from the start and have tried repeatedly to limit its growth.[257] In this, they have been successful. Legislation in 2013 set a new cap on total installed NEM capacity at 5 percent of the peak demand of all customers in each of the three largest utilities' service areas.[258]

There are several reasons the utilities are opposed to net metering. First, regulatory policy that wants to encourage solar energy has required the utilities to pay the customers more for what they put back into the grid than the utilities would pay wholesale providers under a power plant contract. Second, the utilities were caught by surprise by the large uptake of solar installations in the state. Suddenly, the utilities had more power than they could use. Third, the utilities have no significant way to store excess power. So they often are paying top dollar for electricity no one actually uses. Finally, and perhaps most important, NEM is so attractive that it encourages more and more people to install solar more rapidly than they might otherwise. This erodes the historic monopoly role of utilities in providing electricity.

————

All said and done, California's commitment to renewable energy generally, and rooftop solar in particular, has set it apart from other states and placed it with nations such as Germany and Japan, and, increasingly, China, as a world leader. California went about planning and developing its solar programs, particularly the solar initiative, with the clearly expressed goal of a homegrown, self-supporting solar industry over time. The solar program—with its declining block-incentive system, coupled with the federal investment tax incentives, along with net metering— has been successful in achieving the positive public policy outcome.[259]

Business responded positively, not only in terms of ever-improving technology, but also with new business models, such as leasing, instead of selling, rooftop solar units. This meant that customers could have solar without any up-front costs or cash outlays. Government likewise developed new financing mechanisms, such as the Property Assessed Clean Energy Program (PACE) and locally sponsored programs in Berkeley, Sonoma County, and elsewhere. Innovation sparked more innovation, public and private. The growth of solar energy is a California success story that can be emulated elsewhere and undoubtedly will be.

Unlike solar energy, coal, once a major contributor to the state's electrical energy needs, provides less and less of California's electricity production. While California has practically no indigenous coal resources, it has imported coal from neighboring states and run as many as ten coal-fired generating units in the past, mostly used to cogenerate heat and power and located, with the exception of two facilities in Stockton, in the rural and desert areas of Kern and San Bernardino counties.[260]

For many years, Southern California also relied heavily on coal plants built out of state. At its peak, California depended upon nearly 4,600 megawatts of coal power (more than 10 percent of its needs) from six large generating plants: the Navajo Generating Station in Arizona, the Mojave and Reid Gardner generating stations in Nevada, the Four Corners and San Juan generating stations in New Mexico, and the Intermountain Power Plant in Utah.[261] [262] This last power plant, primarily owned by the Los Angeles Department of Water and Power, is today the largest generator of electricity bound for California, with Los Angeles receiving nearly 1,600 megawatts of coal power.[263] [264] In fact, this Utah plant is the biggest single source of electricity consumed by Angelenos.[265]

Reflecting its early concern about global warming and greenhouse gas emissions, the PUC in 2005 adopted a policy resolution that would have the practical effect of reducing and ultimately eliminating the use of coal. The origin of the resolution was the concern throughout the West about many new coal plants in the planning stages. Western Resource Advocates of Denver officials spoke about their concerns to PUC Commissioner Dian Grueneich, her staff, and others. Shortly afterwards, Julie Fitch, the PUC president's chief energy adviser, drafted a policy resolution setting forth an Emissions Performance Standard for power plants producing electricity for California consumers. The adopted resolution was simple in its intent: a death sentence for coal use in California. It established a standard for all generating units of the investor-owned utilities the PUC regulates, stating that the rate of greenhouse gas emissions should be no higher than the rate of those gas emissions from a combined-cycle natural gas plant. No coal plant could meet this emissions standard, which would require a 50 percent cut in greenhouse gases of the out-of-state coal plants. That would end coal use in California.

Accepting the inevitable, Southern California Edison shortly thereafter announced it was closing its Mojave Generating Station, which had used coal transported 242 miles on a coal slurry pipeline from the Navajo Nation Reservation in Arizona.[266] The company subsequently sold its 48 percent ownership of two units of the Four Corners Generating Station in New Mexico.[267] The City of Los Angeles also announced it would wean itself off coal by 2020, replacing it with solar, wind, and other renewable energy sources, as well as greatly increasing its investments in energy efficiency.[268]

Not to be outdone, following a two-day conference sponsored by a leading environmentalist, retired state senator and Stanford law professor Byron Sher, the legislature took up the issue. Governor Schwarzenegger signed Senate Bill 1368, authored by Senate *Pro Tem* Don Perata.[269] The legislation codified the PUC's policy resolution and extended coverage to the state's many municipal utilities.[270] Long-term contracts, however, such as Los Angeles' with the

Intermountain Power Project, means the impact of saying no to coal will not be fully implemented until 2025.

————

By 2006, four years past the energy crisis, California saw clear sailing ahead and was staking its electric energy future on building a limited number of new, combined-cycle natural gas plants, while committing to renewable technologies, chiefly solar and wind, and stressing investments in energy efficiency to dampen demand.

But there were a few misfires in 2006. One occurred when the PUC decided to help combat greenhouse gases through expanded research and demonstration projects housed at the University of California. The commission unanimously voted to create a California Institute for Climate Studies, [271] to be run for a minimum of ten years and supported by utility customers at an annual cost of $60 million; its governing board was to be co-chaired by the presidents of the University of California and the PUC.[272] The idea behind the effort was uncomplicated: greenhouse gases are a growing menace that threatens the well-being of the planet. California is a leader in combating this and has the greatest public university system in the world, renowned for its research in a wide variety of fields. Utility customers are a proxy for the citizenry and should do all they can to combat climate change, and the cost proposed, divided by the number of customers, would be but a few cents a day at most. The institute would use the resources of the university in a coordinated manner in furtherance of a clearly articulated state goal, as stated in Assembly Bill 32.

It was a great idea, perhaps, but its supposed hubris roused the always-simmering quarrel between the agencies and legislature. The view of the PUC, an independent constitutional agency, was that the vote of its five commissioners to set up a new institute to support the state's greenhouse gas goals was legitimate. The legislature felt its feathers ruffle. Deciding on a new institute should be its prerogative, or at least that's what senior energy staffer of the state Senate, Kip Lipper, and colleagues believed. They convinced the leadership, *Pro Tem* Perata and incoming *Pro Tem* Darrell Steinberg, that the executive branch of state government, in this case the PUC, was encroaching on the legislature's terrain. The Office of the Legislative Counsel, whose attorneys advise the legislature, agreed, issuing an opinion saying that the PUC did not have the authority to create the institute and could not force utility ratepayers to pay for it.[273] In the legislators' view, the executive branch is to carry out policies set by the legislature, not to create policies on its own, however meritorious, and then implement them.

Legislators ultimately blocked the PUC-created institute aborning. But under pressure to do something similar, they produced their own version, with a different governing board and functions[274] at an annual cost of $87 million, also paid in large part by utility ratepayers. As the legislative session came to a close, Senators Perata and fellow Democrat Christine Kehoe wrote a legislative version of the PUC's program.[275] The bill made it to Governor Schwarzenegger's desk. He vetoed it, saying he had had enough of the Senate leadership and was not going to further reward them by signing a bill that gutted the PUC's program.[276]

To a major extent, this ended the PUC's ventures into policy arenas where its authority and responsibility were not clear-cut and historic. Perhaps, in hindsight, it was where the battle shifted for the leadership that the PUC, ARB, and the CEC had taken for granted as their own. Or maybe the biggest loser was the UC system, which had seen $60 million in annual research funding appear but not materialize. However, the creativity of the University of California system should never be discounted. Today, almost all of its ten campuses have an institute, school, or center dedicated to studying, developing, and implementing programs to reduce the impact of climate change.[277] What is lacking is a coordinated, cost-effective body to oversee the many, often competitive, efforts.

––––––––––

Another issue that got wide attention was what came to be known as "Smart Meters." Such meters are integral to the successful implementation of a "demand response" program. At its simplest, under a demand response program, business owners and residents agree to lower electricity demand when requested by the utility. As payment for its cooperation, those customers see lower rates. This is commonly used during heat waves, when electric generation capacity cannot handle the air-conditioning demand placed upon it. Instead of a utility having to build an entire new power plant to meet this infrequent demand, the utility has an agreement with some customers that they will reduce their electricity demands when needed by the utility.

The genesis of smart meters in California was a trip in 2004 by PUC President Peevey to visit ENEL, the government-owned national electric utility of Italy. He learned that ENEL officials were installing thirty million new, advanced electric meters throughout the country in order to update the system, provide better, more reliable usage data, and prevent energy theft. The system integrator for the large project was a United States company, IBM, and a major component of the new meters was provided by a San Jose, California, company, Echelon Corporation.

Upon returning to California, Peevey urged the California utilities to study why the Italians had decided to make such a commitment to new meters. Representatives of the three utilities flew to Italy, met with ENEL, and returned home to begin a two-year PUC process of meetings, hearings, and procedures that led to action.

The hearings brought out the many benefits of replacing analog meters, a technology in existence for many years. The older meters, though reliable, could perform only one function—show a customer's total energy consumption over time (usually a one-month billing cycle), but could not do much else. The smart meters, in contrast, could provide two-way communication between the customer and the utility. This occurs over a secure wireless network technology, not via a meter reader going house to house.

In July 2006, the PUC approved smart meters for PG&E, authorizing the company to charge customers $1.7 billion (the ultimate amount topped $2 billion) to upgrade all five million electric meters and four million gas meters. Energy users would now have access to information and greater control over their energy use and bills.

Among other benefits, PG&E could now conduct remote meter reading, pinpoint outages, have remote turn-off/turn-on capability, provide more accurate billing, and prevent energy theft. It could also monitor its electrical load on an hourly basis to more accurately forecast load and identify load centers, enable two-way communication to each customer's meter, and offer varying rates to its customers. This is important, as it can signal smart thermostats, for example. The Northern California utility estimated a demand reduction of 448 megawatts, the equivalent of output from one power plant.

The following April, the PUC approved San Diego Gas & Electric's $572 million smart meter project.[278] The company installed 1.4 million new solid-state electric meters and 900,000 enhanced gas meters.[279] One year later, in September 2008, the PUC approved Southern California Edison's $1.6 billion smart meter project to install 5.3 million new meters.[280] And two years later, the PUC authorized the Southern California Gas Company to retrofit four million gas meters with communicating modules and to replace an additional two million old gas meters with advanced technology.[281] All told, under PUC guidance, the investor-owned utilities have installed, modified, and updated nearly twenty-three million new meters, while several municipal energy and water utilities have installed more than one million more.[282] Energy users absorbed the costs of these meters. However, being able to manage demand ultimately saved them the costs of building new power plants.

All this did not occur without controversy. In some cases, particularly when it came to new or modified gas meters, PUC commissioners were split over whether such meters were cost-effective for consumers. Further, while grudgingly accepting smart meters in some instances, the activist group TURN belittled PG&E efforts on every occasion. Finally, a group of sincere and deeply motivated, mostly San Francisco Bay Area residents, fearing the new meters were unsafe to themselves and the general public health, protested the PUC's actions, repeatedly appearing at PUC meetings to voice their displeasure and calling for a return to use of the older analog meters. In response, the PUC adopted a policy of allowing customers to "opt out" and keep their analog meters. [283] A few thousand utility customers chose to opt out.

In the broader overall policy context set forth in the state's Energy Action Plan as early as 2003, smart meters were the foundation of a vigorous aforementioned demand-response program of which "Time-of-Use" (TOU) pricing is a critical component. This type of pricing, by which electricity can be priced at its true cost of production by hour or some other time interval, is key to the operation of a smart grid, and the state cannot have a meaningful demand-response program without the new meters.

The crucial question, which has held up the spread of TOU pricing to residential electricity users—it already exists for businesses—is whether there should be default TOU rates for all customers and whether, if so, residential customers should be able to opt out. The PUC has kicked this question down the road repeatedly, most recently telling the utilities to design "TOU pilots," and by 2019, design default TOU rates for all residential customers, with no commitment that the PUC would endorse and adopt them.[284]

Still, when all is said and done, it is generally recognized that to have a truly smart grid that operates in the most environmentally positive manner and curbs unnecessary electrical and gas consumption, TOU pricing is necessary. On this, environmentalists, business leaders, public policy advocates, government officials, and most politicians agree in theory, even if they are irresolute in action.

———

Energy efficiency has been a part of California's energy policy for more than forty years. It doesn't have the inherent glamour of zero-emission vehicles or renewable energy. Still, California's greenhouse gas goals could not be achieved without it.

Interest in energy efficiency again came to the fore—via the Energy Action Plan and enactment of Assembly Bill 57, written by Assemblyman Roderick Wright in 2003. Further, legislation in 2005 required the PUC to set targets for "all cost-effective energy efficiency." All told, the decade 2003-2013 saw a remarkable increase in energy efficiency programs and expenditures, a growth beyond what all but the most dedicated supporters of energy efficiency could have wished.

It is fair to ask if this energy efficiency emphasis achieved the goals ascribed to it. According to the PUC and the CEC, with little dispute from observers and practitioners, the savings and benefits to consumers have been large, year in and year out. From 2006 through 2015, the net benefit to consumers has exceeded $2 billion.[285]

All sectors of the California economy have seen energy efficiency benefits in programs that cut across the agricultural, commercial, industrial, residential, and government sectors. Everything from lighting and air-conditioning programs to financing and appliances, to third-party efforts, to custom projects, and government joint efforts are part of the energy efficiency focus. Also included, with large annual expenditures, are workforce education and training, new construction codes and standards, multi-family rebates, marketing, outreach and education, help for low-income homeowners and renters, and a variety of other efforts. Annual energy efficiency expenditures are more than $50 per person statewide, or more than $200 annually for a family of four. This is why it is critical to insure there are true net savings.

The PUC's Evaluation, Measurement and Verification program has been crucial to the understanding of savings and their full extent. This verification process determines in great detail the benefit of each energy efficiency program. This directly affects the earnings of utilities, because they earn not on how many kilowatt-hours they produce, but how many they save.

The impact of California's energy efficiency programs can best be seen by looking at the Rosenfeld curve, named after the pioneer and giant promoter of energy efficiency, the late University of California professor and former CEC Commissioner Arthur Rosenfeld. Since the creation of the California Energy Commission in 1975 and the growth of energy efficiency programs, per capita electricity sales in California have remained flat, while in the rest of the country they have risen 50 percent. The savings have come in all economic sectors, with the greatest in the commercial sector, followed by the residential sector. This pattern is expected to continue well into the future.

The continuing value and importance of energy efficiency can be gleaned further from looking at California's greenhouse gas emission reduction strategies, reflecting the implementation of Assembly Bill 32, the Global Warming Solutions Act. The transportation sector is expected to have the greatest percentage reduction by 2020, some 36 percent, followed by the electricity and gas sectors at 28 percent. More than half of this latter reduction is planned to come from energy efficiency, with almost all the rest coming from the growth of renewables, such as solar, wind, and biomass.

In 2013, the San Onofre Nuclear Generating Station in San Diego County unexpectedly closed permanently, leaving 2,200 megawatts of replacement electricity—20 percent of total regional usage—needing to be found for Southern Californians. After thinking through options in light of the greenhouse gas goals of the state, the PUC decision on replacement power appears to many as a radical idea: to replace one-half of the output of a massive 2,200-megawatt nuclear plant that ran twenty-four hours a day, seven days a week, with energy efficiency programs. Yet this is the course the state has chosen, and its success seems likely.

Profiles in Leadership
Byron Sher—Influential Environmental Champion

© Robert Durell 1998,
Los Angeles Times

Born in St. Louis, Missouri, in 1928, son of a politically active lawyer, Byron Sher graduated from Washington University in his hometown and later Harvard Law School. Sher taught at several universities before migrating west, ultimately coming to Stanford Law School as a professor. Active in governance of the university, environmental concerns prompted him to jump into local politics and led to his election to the Palo Alto City Council, where he served two terms as its mayor before being elected to the state Assembly in 1980. He served sixteen years in the lower house and then was elected to the state Senate in 1996, serving two terms before retiring in December 2004 due to term limits.

No one wrote as much environmental and energy legislation as did Sher in his twenty-four years in the legislature. His record is legendary: Assembly Bill 1362, the nation's first law preventing toxic contamination from leaking underground storage tanks (1983); AB 2595, the California Clean Air Act (1987); AB 939, the Integrated Waste Management Act (1989); AB 21, the Safe Drinking Water Act (1989); AB 3995, the first legislation requiring electric utilities to use renewable energy (1990); AB 653, to preserve free-flowing parts of seven state rivers (1993); SB 527, the California Climate Action Registry, to measure and record greenhouse gas inventories (2001); SB 1078, the first explicit and measurable renewable energy standard (2002); SB 20, California's e-waste program (2003); and SB 23, which greatly expanded California's waste recycling program (2003).

Sher took great care to make sure his Silicon Valley constituents were responsible for computer recycling programs to ensure that some of the polluting products of the information age, such as mercury, did not contaminate the water supply or landfills. Perhaps Sher's signature achievement was his solid waste bill in 1989 that reduced by more than 50 percent the amount of solid wastes going into landfills. To many people, Sher was "Mr. Recycling." He also took special pride in his efforts on energy efficiency, development of renewable energy and the growth of the renewable industry to its leading position in California today.

In tribute to Sher, the main auditorium of the California EPA head-quarters, where many hard battles are still fought today at monthly ARB board meetings, bears his name.

Arthur H. Rosenfeld—Father of Energy Efficiency

Courtesy of the Lawrence Berkeley National Library

A very small event kicked Art Rosenfeld into his everlasting devotion to energy efficiency. One Friday night, he was working late at his office at the Lawrence Berkeley National Laboratory during the first Arab oil embargo in November 1973. Rosenfeld, doing a brief calculation, realized that if his office lights stayed on all weekend, about five gallons of oil, or its natural-gas equivalent, would be burned to keep the office lit. His was one of twenty offices on his floor, and he was one of the few occupants who turned off his lights when departing.

In a burst of inspiration, he decided to switch off the lights in the other nineteen offices. But he had difficulty finding the proper switches in all the other offices. Some were behind books, others hidden by file cabinets, bookcases, and wall hangings. He finally succeeded in turning off all the lights and decided it was time for the laboratory and the University of California to start conserving energy in an organized manner. He would devote the balance of his professional life to promoting energy conservation and efficiency.

In a way, this was a radical career change. Rosenfeld earned a Bachelor of Science degree from Virginia Polytechnic Institute at age eighteen in 1944 and, after serving in the Navy, went to the University of Chicago, where, as the last student of famed Nobel laureate Enrico Fermi, he earned his doctorate in physics in 1954. He then joined the physics department of the University of California, Berkeley and oversaw the Nobel Prize-winning particle physics group of Luis Alvarez at the Lawrence Berkeley National Laboratory. Though he always kept an office and affiliation with the Berkeley laboratory, he left his position there in 1974, shortly after experiencing his energy efficiency epiphany.

Changing his career emphasis, Rosenfeld co-founded and directed the energy efficient buildings program at the Berkeley laboratory. Much technical work ensued, leading to the development of such products as high-frequency solid-state ballasts for fluorescent lamps and the US Department of Energy's computer program for energy

119

analysis and design of buildings. In 1976, he brought to Governor Brown's attention the inefficiency of the common refrigerator. Brown responded by asking the CEC to immediately develop new standards for refrigerators and freezers. It did, and new refrigerator use of electricity was reduced by 80 percent over the next several years. This led to the federal government developing similar standards, implemented by the Department of Energy.

In 1979, Rosenfeld co-founded the American Council for an Energy Efficient Economy, a national nonprofit promoting efficiency nationally. In the mid-1980s, he started what has led to one of his signature accomplishments, the Urban Heat Island Research Project at the Lawrence Berkeley National Laboratory. The research examined how to switch to cooler roofs and pavements. This has led to today's general recognition that white roofs can reduce global warming by reflecting heat back into space.

For his efforts, he received in 1986 the Leo Szilard Award for Physics in the Public Interest and two years later co-founded the University of California-based California Institute for Energy and the Environment. During much of the 1990s, he served as a senior adviser to the US Department of Energy, specializing in energy efficiency and renewable energy, and he was known as an early and ardent supporter of rooftop solar energy.

In 2000, California Governor Gray Davis appointed him to the CEC; Governor Schwarzenegger reappointed him in 2005. Rosenfeld took responsibility for much of the CEC's public interest energy research program, which had an annual budget of more than $80 million and, of course, included working to insure greater efficiency standards for buildings and appliances, such as large-screen televisions.

Rosenfeld received innumerable awards, including in 2006 the Enrico Fermi Award, given to him by President George W. Bush for his lifetime of achievement, ranging from scientific discoveries in experimental nuclear and particle physics to innovations in science, technology, and public policy. Upon his passing away in 2017, Governor Brown told the Los Angeles Times, "He gave validation to the very unorthodox notion that economic growth could be decoupled from energy growth. He was really the guru of efficiency."

CHAPTER 10

YIN/YANG

The second decade of the twentieth century ushered in a bit of the old—a governor in his 70s, again wearing the mantle of leadership. He focused on an energy policy that implemented an aggressive climate change agenda. The road was not smooth. Entrenched interests sought to overturn the state's pioneering greenhouse gas reduction law, thwart the renewal of the state's energy research and development program, and curb any effort to reduce dependency upon polluting fossil fuels for vehicles.

Edmund G. Brown Jr. was elected to his third term as California governor in November 2010, twenty-eight years after completing his second term as governor. He defeated Republican Meg Whitman 53.4 percent to 40.6 percent in a hard-fought campaign, despite her outspending him $178.5 million ($144 million from Whitman's personal funds) to $36.5 million. [286] Brown's first priority was restoring the state to fiscal stability following years of economic chaos, reflected in massive budget cuts, state employee layoffs and furloughs, and a declining economy with growing unemployment. In short, when Brown took office January 1, 2011, the Golden State had a $27 billion deficit and had lost much of its luster.

In the same election, California voters rejected an initiative campaign to gut AB 32. As noted earlier, in 2006, the California legislature had passed, and Governor Schwarzenegger signed into law, AB 32. The landmark legislation was recognized worldwide and committed California to steadily reduce greenhouse gases annually. While the environmental community and many others in and outside of government loved the statute, the energy industry felt the opposite.

Two years later, the national economy cratered, experiencing its biggest decline since the Great Depression of the 1930s. California was particularly hard hit, with unemployment (12.4 percent in November 2010) much greater than the national average (9.8 percent).

Enemies of the global climate law saw their opportunity. Two Texas oil companies with big investments in California, Valero Energy Corporation and Tesoro Corporation, qualified a ballot initiative, Proposition 23, for the November 2010 election. [287] [288] Cleverly, the initiative didn't seek to kill AB 32 but to simply "suspend it" until the unemployment rate dropped to 5.5 percent or below for a minimum of a year.

The Texans had money and a simple message: "Now is not the time for stricter environmental rules and regulations. Now is the time to relax them and to create jobs."

Early polling showed a majority of the public was sympathetic to the jobs argument. A survey by the Public Policy Institute of California in July 2010 found two-thirds of Californians in favor of AB 32, with a majority—54 percent to 42 percent—saying the state should wait to take further action to reduce emissions until the state economy and jobs situation improved.[289] The Proposition 23 advertising campaign was proving to be effective.

The environmental community was alarmed. Working with Joe Caves of the Conservation Strategy Group in Sacramento, representatives of these groups approached the Los Angeles firm of Winner & Mandabach Campaigns, seeking advice and counsel. It was clear from the outset that an aggressive campaign dependent upon large-scale fundraising was critical if Proposition 23 were to be defeated. Up stepped Tom Steyer, a San Francisco billionaire investment banker with a strong environmental commitment.[290] Soon there was an emerging campaign team: Charles Winner, Paul Mandabach and Steyer, with former Clinton administration staff member Chris Lehane very involved.

Early on, the "no" campaign realized its cause would be greatly strengthened if the public leadership of the campaign were bipartisan. Governor Schwarzenegger sought the support of George Shultz, President Ronald Reagan's secretary of state and a resident scholar at Stanford University.[291] Shultz and Steyer became co-chairs of the No on 23 campaign, with Shultz speaking out about why suspending Proposition 23 was bad for California and implying that the popular former governor, Ronald Reagan, would feel likewise.

The "no" campaign was remarkably successful in its broad appeals and garnered the support of a wide range of Californians, ultimately including both the Democratic and Republican candidates for governor, Jerry Brown and Meg Whitman, as well as outgoing Governor Schwarzenegger. When Governor Schwarzenegger learned that the anti-32 forces qualified their initiative for the ballot, he noted: "The effort to suspend AB 32 is the work of greedy oil companies who want to keep polluting our state and making profits."[292]

That was pretty much the theme of the anti-23 campaign. As events unfolded, the strategy of the Proposition 23 opposition was simple—attack as major polluters the two Texas companies, Valero and Tesoro, funding the "yes" campaign. Of note was the No on 23 campaign strategy to keep other major oil companies, such as Chevron, Exxon, and Shell, from joining the "yes" campaign with significant resources. The strategic decision was to label the initiative's supporters as two Texas oil companies attempting to dictate California energy policy for their own financial gain. The strategy worked, and the two Texas companies found themselves isolated. Other major oil companies, such as California-headquartered Chevron, stayed neutral, as did Exxon and Shell.[293]

Further, much of the California business community either stayed uninvolved or opposed Prop. 23. The Los Angeles Business Council, the San Francisco Chamber of Commerce, the California Black Chamber of Commerce, and the Latino Business Association all campaigned for a no vote.   They joined a wide range of more traditional interest groups: the health and welfare community, such as the American Lung Association and others concerned with asthma, faith-based groups, AARP, and hundreds of other organizations. Celebrities Leonardo DiCaprio, Robert Redford, Edward James Olmos, and James Cameron spoke out against the proposition.

Fundraising against Prop 23, led by Steyer, was prodigious. He alone contributed $5.05 million, while Tesoro and Valero together contributed only $5.6 million to the yes side. The no campaign raised $32 million, most of it by Steyer and friends, and outspent by more than 2 to 1 the supporters of Proposition 23, who ultimately included billionaires Charles and David Koch.

The clever anti-23 ads focused on renewable energy's promise, health concerns, dependence on costly oil, and loss of jobs in the clean-technology industry, while tagging the two Texas companies as big polluters. The *Los Angeles Times* provided a tally of the prodigious No on 23 effort, noting: "opponents mustered 3,200 volunteers, made 2.8 million phone calls to voters, sent out 3.4 million pieces of mail, made 379,676 on-campus contacts with college students, and operated a computerized outreach program that identified and contacted 481,000 voters, and showered voters with 900,000 get-out-the vote phone calls and text messages in the last three days."[294]

Election night saw Proposition 23 go down to overwhelming defeat, losing 62 to 38 percent.[295] In what Californians hoped would be a precursor to a national debate on climate change policy, Prop 23 tracking polls days before the election indicated that the margin of votes by moderate and liberal Republicans against the initiative was 44 percent to 36 percent in favor, and among Republican women it was even greater, 46 percent against to 33 percent in favor.

National Environmental Defense Fund President Fred Krupp hailed the victory in a larger context: "Almost ten million Californians got a chance to vote and sent a clear message that they want a clean energy future. And this was during the financial meltdown that began in 2008. There has never been anything this big. It is going to send a signal to other parts of the country and beyond."[296]

The election result was a validation by the electorate of the goals and thrust of AB 32, even in difficult economic times. Yet without the fundraising prowess of Steyer, the clever, hard-hitting media ads of Winner & Mandabach, and the bipartisan support for the No on 23 side led by Republicans Schwarzenegger, Shultz, and Whitman (who was prodded by the governor to oppose the initiative), the outcome could have been different.

Since the defeat of Proposition 23, there has not been any successful effort to reduce the impact of AB 32, nor has there been any major effort to alter or overturn the state's other pioneering environmental and energy laws and regulations. California has signaled its aggressive intent to stand up against federal government attempts to dilute its laws and regulations. The state talks tough, will sue the federal government at any turn, and use its considerable stable of elected officials to influence the Trump administration. Since President Trump's election, California has been even more aggressive. Still, pitched battles between the national government and a state, even

California, do not present good odds for a state overall. Californians are worried. The California experience suggests that people can have both a prosperous economy and an enhanced environment. Will this continue unimpeded?

———

When Jerry Brown was elected governor in 2010, his first priority was fixing the state's enormous fiscal problems. In 2012, in a practically unprecedented move, Governor Brown sought and sponsored a statewide voter initiative to temporarily raise state taxes, with the focus being to sharply increase the personal income tax on high-income earners, though the sales tax was also raised slightly. The majority of voters, believing and trusting Brown, voted for the measure. This was a singular triumph for the then-74-year-old governor's credibility, and it allowed him to turn his attention to other issues.

The most pressing to him was climate change and its related energy and environmental issues, though Brown did champion two megabillion-dollar projects—the construction of a high-speed bullet train between Los Angeles and San Francisco via the San Joaquin Valley and the construction of two massive tunnels under the Bay Delta to transport water from north to south.[297] As of this writing, both projects remain mired in controversy and are bitterly opposed by various constituencies.

Brown inherited strong leadership at the major energy and environmental agencies under his command. Mary Nichols, who had served as ARB chair during his second term as governor, 1979 to 1983, once again had been appointed to the air board chair by Schwarzenegger. Brown retained her. Michael Peevey, who was appointed to the PUC by Gray Davis and reappointed by Schwarzenegger, was kept as president. Robert Weisenmiller, who had been named chairman of the CEC by Schwarzenegger, was retained, as was Robert Foster, chair of the California Independent System Operator (CAISO). Foster was mayor of Long Beach and a former president of Southern California Edison. Augmented by the governor's office personnel, principal among them Nancy McFadden, a former senior vice president of PG&E and now Brown's chief staffer, the group came to compose the energy principals. The group met monthly throughout Brown's third term, sometimes with the governor present, and was instrumental in shaping and guiding the coordinated policies and initiatives of their respective agencies.

Even before his 2010 inauguration, Brown had endorsed most of the energy-environmental policies and initiatives of his predecessor and, in fact, in some instances chose to double-down on them. He enthusiastically endorsed and sought to expand the state's commitment to renewable energy, primarily rooftop solar and central generating plants, as well as the ARB's initial efforts to create a cap-and-trade system of pollution allowances.

Undergirding many of these programs was California's energy research and demonstration efforts, funding of which was made possible by the PUC's imposition of the public goods charge, paid by every investor-owned utility customer in the state. The ten-year-old program, absolutely vital to the California Energy Commission's research efforts, needed to be reauthorized in 2011. While there was majority support in the legislature for the program, the extension required a two-thirds vote in both legislative houses, which it did not receive.

Brown, frustrated, turned to the PUC president and asked if the commission on its own could continue the research and development program. Penned to the bottom of the governor's letter was a note saying, "When the Legislature fails, the Executive prevails." The PUC, with some modest changes, including changing the name to the Electric Program Investment Charge (EPIC), renewed the program under its umbrella in a unanimous decision in May 2012.

Administered by the CEC and utilities, the initial budget of EPIC was $162 million in 2013, with $128 million going to the CEC for applied research, technology demonstration and deployment, market facilitation, and program administration. Each of the utilities received amounts proportional to their size for technology demonstration and deployment. In future years, beginning in 2015, the total budget was to be increased by annual increases in the federal consumer price index, and total spending for the years 2015-17 is expected to exceed $500 million.

Thus, the state program of research, development and demonstration in renewables and their integration with the grid, a focus on customer products and services, and ways to modernize the grid and its operations—all work to be done by the utilities—has moved forward. However, first the EPIC program had to survive a challenge to its existence.

Southern California Edison, even while its staff was working with other utilities, the CEC, and the PUC to implement EPIC, filed suit in the state court of appeals, seeking to kill the program. Its lawsuit claimed the PUC had exceeded its authority by creating EPIC after the legislature had failed to continue the program by statute.

The governor's office and the PUC president tried to convince Edison to withdraw the lawsuit, pointing out that the entire state research and demonstration effort in electricity was being jeopardized. Edison officials refused, claiming they were acting to protect their customers from a rate increase. They claimed the PUC has too much power already and, left unchallenged, the PUC would essentially have the right to tax for any purpose that it could assert was beneficial to utility customers.

The Second District Court of Appeal denied Edison's lawsuit in 2014, ruling the fee did not constitute a tax, and the company chose not to appeal the decision to the state Supreme Court. A powerful state agency prevailed once again.

The state has recognized for some time that the growth of renewable technologies, such as solar and wind, produced a set of new challenges along with opportunities. The most obvious problem is that solar and wind power are intermittent technologies, producing electricity only some of the time. Thus, reliability is a concern; back-up power must be available for homeowners, businesses, and other users. Hence, the interest in energy storage has grown alongside the growth in solar and wind energy.

In 2010, Assemblywoman Nancy Skinner, a champion of solar energy, introduced Assembly Bill 2514, which, when signed into law by Governor Schwarzenegger shortly before leaving office, would once again burnish California's image as a leader in twenty-first century energy policy. The law required the PUC, by March 1, 2012, to open a proceeding to determine appropriate procurement targets for energy storage by the three large investor-owned utilities, Commissioner

Carla J. Peterman summed up the importance of the law and the PUC's action: "I believe energy storage has great potential to help us address grid reliability and renewables integration issues. This decision is an important and appropriate step … [toward] integrating renewable energy from solar and wind into the overall electricity mix … by October 1, 2013."

The PUC's work on the project, spearheaded by Peterman and announced that month, set a target of 1,325 megawatts of total energy storage for the utilities, with targets increased gradually to 2020, with full installation of storage capacity to occur no later than 2024. Included in the program are community-choice aggregators and electric service providers, who, combined, represent less than 15 percent of the nonmunicipal-utility electricity consumers in the state. This number is rapidly increasing. The result would meet the law's intent: increased reliability, reduction of peak demand, reduced demand for transmission and distribution system upgrades, and decreased pollution through reducing greenhouse gas emissions.

The storage plan, the largest of its kind in the nation and worldwide, is a game-changer and will allow homeowners and businesses to better manage their energy use and, ultimately, in many cases, free consumers from dependence, except in emergencies, upon the grid. Already its impact has been felt, with the announcement in 2015 that Tesla, the electric-car company building a gigantic battery factory outside Reno, Nevada, would also provide batteries for energy storage for homeowners and businesses. In 2016, Tesla took a further step in integrating electric vehicles and battery storage by acquiring the rooftop solar installer SolarCity.

The 2013 decision set specific goals by utility, requiring PG&E and Edison to procure 580 megawatts each of storage by 2020 and for SDG&E to procure 165 megawatts. The nonutility-electricity providers are required to meet one percent of their peak load by energy storage by 2020. California policies in energy storage will help to fundamentally alter the 100-year-old utility economic model as consumer reliance on the utility drops and, in some cases, vanishes.

Californians have realized for years that the world would not be able to address air quality in general or greenhouse gas reductions specifically without decreasing dependence on oil as a transportation fuel. The state's vision is that by 2050, fuel cell, electric, and hybrid light-duty vehicles will make up almost the entire California auto fleet. Because cars drove essentially 100 percent on gasoline in 2006, and as owners are keeping their autos for an average of eleven and a half years,[298] the goal is quite a stretch.

California tried to start down the electric-car path early by adopting its first zero-emission auto regulation in 1990. The requirement was for all large automakers to offer 2 percent of their new cars as electric by the 1998 model year. The automakers didn't even bother fighting this rule. They thought it was too ridiculous, from both technology and cost points of view. Very few automakers brought electric cars to market. Of those that did, GM's EV1 was beautiful and sleek. But it was very expensive and realistically had a forty-mile range. In the end, the automakers' reality prevailed, and the rule was pulled back.

Still, the automakers knew that the ARB sometimes backs off, but never goes away. This is part of the regulatory certainty in which California prides itself. The automakers also knew that as California goes, so often goes the world. Internally, some of the automakers turned to how best to commercialize zero-emission vehicles (ZEVs).

California is the nation's largest market for cars and light-duty trucks, with more than twenty-five million registered vehicles. The state had nearly 50 percent of all ZEV sales in the country as of October 2016, with the nine other states with ZEV mandates standing at 13 percent. Sales are expected to increase in 2017 with the launch of three new lower-cost models—the Tesla Model 3, the Toyota Prius Prime and the Chevy Bolt EV, the 2017 Motor Trend Car of the Year.[299]

To attain clean air for every Californian and to reach the statewide greenhouse gas emission goal of 80 percent below 1990 levels by 2050, nearly 100 percent of new vehicle sales by 2040 will have to be ZEVs. The ARB has set a complex, milestone-laden path to assure that happens.

During the transition, while most people will continue to need gasoline fuel, another strong leadership position for California is its low-carbon fuel standard, which is probably its most controversial program. The ZEV rule and cap-and-trade initiatives are accepted calmly compared with low-carbon fuels.

The low-carbon fuel standard requires transportation fuels cut their carbon intensity by 10 percent by 2020. Today, California gasoline is already much cleaner than it is in much of the rest of the world. Achieving another 10 percent will be a real effort, and the path to get there isn't clear. But the performance standard is in place and unlikely to change. The electric power and automotive and industrial sectors have all accepted and responded to large, difficult sector reductions in greenhouse gas emissions. The oil industry is the last man standing in fighting back, always punching, sometimes winning. But many in California view the oil industry as a dead man walking and believe the regulations will once again lead the way to a low-carbon economy.

The most successful electric car to date, in sales as well as aesthetic and technical excellence, is the Tesla. The man behind the Tesla, Elon Musk, comes from a family of South African entrepreneurs, engineers, and glamorous risk-takers. After immigrating to Canada and wandering down to the United States, Musk moved to California, enrolling at Stanford University, intending to get a doctorate in energy physics. But the academy was too slow-paced for him, and he dropped out to go into business.

First, he created Zip2, which he sold for more than $300 million in 1999. At the same time, he created PayPal, acquired by eBay for $1.5 billion in 2000. In 2002, SpaceX was launched, and in 2008 Musk became CEO of Tesla. Today he is putting the finishing touches on the biggest battery plant in the world, near Reno, Nevada. The batteries will power his electric cars and also commercial and residential rooftop solar projects installed by SolarCity, the largest solar rooftop company in the United States, which is now part of Tesla. In 2013, Musk started funding hyperloop projects, which he envisions transporting people from Los Angeles to San Francisco in thirty minutes. Musk's companies have created more than 20,000 direct jobs in California, and more indirectly.

As previously noted, California's 2006 Global Warming Solutions Act, AB 32, calls for many measures to reduce greenhouse gases in a multitude of sectors. One controversial feature is a cap-and-trade program for greenhouse gases. In fact, cap and trade was such a polarizing program that it wasn't even an explicit part of the bill. But the law allowed ARB to implement cap and trade, and it did.

Cap and trade, also known as emissions trading, is a flexible way to reduce emissions mandated under a cap. For example, assume Company X has a mandate to reduce its greenhouse gas emissions to 100 tons. Traditional regulatory requirements would explicitly spell out what control technology Company X had to install. Under cap and trade, Company X could choose to install controls, or it could look for emissions reductions made by other companies and "buy" those emission reductions. The regulatory agency would get what it wants—reduced emissions. Company X is able to comply through purchasing reductions for sale at a cheaper price than installing its own controls. As the cap tightens, Company X will have to eventually control its own emissions. But cap and trade is set up to encourage the cheapest reductions to occur first.

Theoretically, this means that greenhouse gases are reduced at the lowest overall cost to society. This was a major move away from strict reliance on mandatory command and control policies, heretofore the prime methods used to curtail pollution. But cap and trade just doesn't sit right with many people. They see it as selling a license to pollute, even if overall emissions are reduced.

The California cap-and-trade program sets a statewide limit on polluting sources responsible for about 85 percent of California's greenhouse gas emissions and is the first in the nation to apply to multiple sectors of the economy. The program began in 2013 for electricity generators and large industrial facilities, such as oil refineries and cement plants, and was extended in 2015 to transportation and natural gas. The program is now linked to similar trading programs in the Canadian provinces of Quebec and Ontario, and other states and provinces are expected to join over time.

California started auctioning off emissions allowances and reductions to large greenhouse gas emitters in November 2012. The money collected funded smaller reduction projects, energy efficiency for low-income housing, greenhouse gas transportation reduction programs such as electric vehicles, the building of sustainable communities, public transit improvements, new high-speed rail, and other environmental programs.

Over the first three years of cap and trade, the state collected $3.5 billion in auction revenues. Some people decry cap and trade as steadily increasing the already high cost of doing business in California. They also point to the 2012 Clean Energy Jobs Act, which estimated that by closing a major tax loophole, upward of $500 million a year would be provided to fund clean-energy projects and schools, and this would create more than 10,000 jobs annually. To date, fewer than 2,000 jobs have been created, and much of the money remains unspent. The program's biggest sponsors, state Senate President Kevin de León and environmental leader Tom Steyer remain sanguine about the initiative's ultimate success. And there is cause for optimism, though the slowness of new programs at all levels of government is too typical in today's bureaucratic world.

2016 saw agreement on a particularly significant piece of legislation—that California will reduce greenhouse gases by 40 percent by 2030 compared with its 1990 level. The bill setting out the new reduction target was again authored by now-retired state Senator Fran Pavley and the bill's number, SB 32, has symbolic significance, coming ten years after passage, in 2006, of AB 32. This new reduction is being targeted by the Trump administration, which claims California will need a new waiver to enact these more stringent emission controls.

Another issue unresolved in 2016 was whether the California Independent System Operator (CAISO) would become more of a Western states regional grid by merging it with PacifiCorp, the large private utility operating in several Western states—Oregon, Washington, Idaho, Utah, Montana, Wyoming, and a small slice of Northern California. Proponents of such a consolidation believe that a regional approach to grid operations would increase the flow of power between the states, be more economical, and spur the development of more renewable energy throughout the West. For example, connecting the grid would likely spur new wind power in Wyoming, because now California could be its destination.

Some environmental groups, particularly the Sierra Club, and building-trades unions in California view such an expansion warily. The environmental groups in opposition fear that an integrated and merged Western grid could mean more coal power would come to California. Some unions fear that they could lose prospective construction jobs to other states, where new projects would be constructed more cheaply than in California. Governor Brown and legislative leaders decided to postpone action on creating a regional grid until 2017 or later, disappointing not only builders and developers, but some environmental groups, who saw a merged Western grid as a progressive step in building a more vibrant and vital regional grid that would enhance the further development of renewable energy.

California also saw its world leadership role further challenged by Germany, the home of some of the world's highest-performing automobiles, which announced initial steps to ban the manufacturing of gasoline-fueled cars by 2030. Such a ban by a country that is a world leader in producing technically advanced automobiles will undoubtedly affect the whole world's marketplace for cars. This announcement comes only a few years after Chancellor Angela Merkel proclaimed that Germany would end its reliance on nuclear energy by closing all its nuclear plants—a very bold step environmentally to many, though the consequences in terms of greenhouse gas emissions are unclear.

Finally, 2016 saw the continuing strong support by Californians for curbing global warming, even independent of the federal government. According to a statewide poll by the Public Policy Institute of California released in January 2017, the vast majority of California adults—81 percent—believe global warming is a serious threat to the state's economy and quality of life.[300]

Californians heavily support (68 percent) the aggressive stance of SB 32, calling for a 40 percent reduction in greenhouse gas emissions below 1990 levels by 2030. Further, they are willing to pay more for a cleaner, more greenhouse gas-free environment, with 56 percent saying that to reduce global warming, "they are willing to pay more for electricity if it is generated by renewable sources like solar or wind," according to the PPIC poll. They (59 percent) also fully expect gasoline prices will rise as well.

All these polling numbers suggest that large percentages of state residents will continue to support state and local actions to curb global warming today and in the years to come.

Profile in Leadership
Tom Steyer—Billionaire Funder of Environmental Issues

© Ann Cusack 2014,
Los Angeles Times

Tom Steyer is the éminence grise behind some of the strong environmental movements and successful ballot initiatives in the state. Over the years, his support has made the difference in statewide issues, from saving AB 32, to dedicating tax monies, to energy-efficiency upgrades for California schools. Since Trump's election, he has broadened his activities throughout the nation primarily through activities of his nonprofit organization, NextGen America, which seeks to encourage environmental activism in younger people.

Yet, it was not always thus. A native of New York City's Upper East Side, his father was a senior partner at the prestigious, old-line law firm of Sullivan & Cromwell. Steyer had a privileged youth. After attending the exclusive Manhattan boys school, Buckley, he was at the top of his graduating class at Phillips Exeter Academy. Then it was Yale, Wall Street and Stanford Business School. In 1986 Steyer created his own company, Farallon Capital Management. The company, headquartered in San Francisco, was a great success, and Steyer became a billionaire.

He always had a strong interest in public policy issues and the environment and was drawn to politics and social activism. But for a moment in time he had a bit of a double life, committed to community and social justice while his company, Farallon, was criticized for investing in Canadian tar sand fields.

Steyer underwent an epiphany, moving from a prime focus on making money into public policy and politics. He started to back out of Farallon and began contributing large sums to Democratic candidates for various offices. By 2010, he teamed with George Shultz, the venerable alumnus of the Nixon and Reagan administrations, to lead the effort to defeat Prop 23. This worked; the effort to retreat from California's pioneering global warming law was overwhelmingly defeated in a statewide vote.

In 2012, Steyer, moved by the need to sharply reduce greenhouse gas emissions worldwide, began to focus his attention on defeating the proposed Keystone XL pipeline, which would bring oil from Alberta's tar sands to the United States. Steyer aggressively campaigned against the pipeline, spending chunks of his money to defeat pro-pipeline candidates in other states. In the end, President Obama, vetoed the pipeline. President Trump reversed the Obama decision and gave the pipeline the green light in early 2017. The fight goes on.

Steyer has become a major political player nationally, with a willingness to use his money for environmental and other causes he holds dear. He has made a big difference, affecting outcomes both in California and nationally.

Epilogue

Bipartisanship on climate has been a theme throughout this book. A most recent and relevant example of bipartisan leadership was Governor Jerry Brown's successful campaign to re-authorize California's cap and trade program and extend its life from 2020 until 2030. A cap and trade program requires permits to emit greenhouse gases. By 2017, prices for allowances were falling. Companies were not complying vigorously, because the program was set to expire in 2020. "Lame Duck-itis" was influencing behavior.

Since the California legislature has a Democrat majority in both houses, reauthorizing the program wouldn't seem to be in question. But over the years, the program had been challenged on several fronts, including on the grounds that it was essentially a carbon tax. All taxes require a two-thirds vote in the legislature. The original law had passed with a simple majority. Although the law had survived the legal challenges regarding taxation to date, Governor Brown insisted that the reauthorization act had to pass the legislature by two-thirds in order to slam the door shut once and for all against legality challenges.

Senate leader Kevin De Leon was doubtful this could happen. He called it a unicorn bill, since it would be a miracle if Governor Brown got his two-thirds vote. In fact, voting on the legislation had to be postponed several times because there wasn't a two-thirds vote to be had. Some Democrats and most Republicans opposed it. The Governor doggedly button-holed many legislators individually, found out what they wanted in the bill, and insisted on fixes that would assure the right number of votes. He personally testified at the bill's Senate Environmental Committee hearing and sat there for four hours, listening to testimony and giving an impassioned speech about the importance of climate action for the sake of the next generation.

Former Republican Governors Pete Wilson and Arnold Schwarzenegger endorsed the bill. George Schultz, Ronald Reagan's secretary of state, wrote a letter saying he was positive President Reagan would have approved the measure. And, in the end, AB 398, the extension of cap and trade, passed with a two-thirds vote, which included eight Republicans.

At exactly the same time, summer 2017, President Trump was trying to pass a new health care law in the US Congress. Even though Republicans were in the majority in both houses, and he only needed a majority vote, the President did not manage to corral the needed votes to either pass a new bill or kill the current law. As of July 2017, no new health care legislation of any kind was passed nationally.

Part of this difference in outcomes can be credited to the leaders themselves. Governor Brown was experienced and tireless in his work to pass the cap and trade extension. President Trump was politically inexperienced and half-hearted in his work with the Congress.

But it is also fair to note the probable influence of California's new statewide primary process for state and federal elections on the cap and trade outcome. In most state primary elections, Republicans vote for a Republican and Democrats vote for a Democrat. The top vote getter on each side oppose one another in the general election.

In California, every candidate for state or congressional office is listed on a single Primary Election ballot. All voters choose the candidate of their choice from the same ballot. The top two primary vote winners advance to the General Election. In practice, this means that sometimes two Republicans or two Democrats face off against one another in the general election. This one ballot primary tends to favor candidates who hold more middle positions on issues. The process does not favor the election of extremists at either end.

Significantly lowering carbon emissions will create a different world, one that can survive and thrive with a solid foundation of support from visionary leaders and an enlightened public. Key elements, put into place and managed by leaders committed to the public's well-being, can build long-term environmental policy that can be emulated. Although every sector of society must take responsibility in its own way, a government driving carbon reductions is essential to the success of a plan that will endure long into the future.

None of the attributes of California climate leadership is unique; together they serve as a model for other jurisdictions, from counties to countries. The core strategy of bipartisanship was honed over smog. The opaque smog in the 1940s and 1950s did not discriminate between conservatives and liberals, or wealthy and low-income residents; it made the eyes and throats of everyone burn and exacerbated asthma and bronchial attacks among children of all social and economic classes.

Calls for help came from every corner of society. It has been Republicans and Democrats, from governors to agency staff and voters, who have since created, endorsed, and enshrined into law aggressive environmental regulations to clean up the air we breathe. And along the way, hundreds of thousands of jobs have been created across industries, from solar systems and wind power to electric cars and more.

The party in power can change, but political systems need to be stable, accountable, and responsive to their people. The goal is to build momentum over decades and generations, to build the pillars of support higher and stronger so that no future anti-climate change ideologues can chip away or topple the environmental edifice that has been built.

California has shown that keeping up with climate change could not have succeeded without capitalizing on the asset of high-quality government agencies and the world-class universities with which the state has been blessed. California's agencies need a good deal of technical competence, energy, and other science expertise, legal acumen, and credible laboratory research. Symbiotically, the state's outstanding academic institutions educate their students deeply within these disciplines. Many of the universities have institutes that specialize in climate change work, such as the UCLA Center for Climate Science, the Stanford Precourt Institute for Energy, UC Berkeley's Energy and Climate Institute, the Linde Center for Global Environmental Science at CalTech, and many others. These programs people the state and local agencies with the intellectual capital and knowledge of new technology vital to addressing climate change.

Climate experts and other scientists from around the world have come to the Golden State to work at universities, government laboratories, research institutions, and Silicon Valley corporations to focus on combatting global warming. This has brought about a bonus effect: California's state budget has realized many billions of dollars from increased tax revenues when successful entrepreneurs monetized their achievements.

How energy and environmental agencies get the funding to operate is important, too. Rather than annual funding from the general fund, which ebbs and flows with economic downturns and upturns, agencies mandated to develop energy and environmental policy were established to withstand such competition for budget dollars through some near-autonomous sustainable funding based on polluter-pays concepts such as emissions permits and fees.

Developing accurate data in environmental debates often will reinforce or turn the tide of public opinion. Accuracy offsets "fake news" about climate change and global warming that now emanates from the nation's capital. Real benefits should be emphasized in research projects, such as improved health for individuals, lower public health costs to the state, ecosystem improvements linked to sustainability, indirect rise in property values, and the overall community benefits of new jobs and industries.

Obviously, not everyone has been on board the environmental train. Oil companies, as discussed, have little to gain from more zero-emission vehicles. Carmakers in Detroit, Tokyo, and elsewhere loathe having to produce cars for California—the largest vehicle market in the country, which has ever-stricter emission regulations than elsewhere in the United States. Arguments about the high cost of environmental protection are relentless and often have been effective at stalling laws and regulations.

At the moment, the auto manufacturers have a US president who is sympathetic to their complaints and, along with his head of the federal EPA, wants to accede to the desires of the auto manufacturers and override California's tough emission standards. But California leaders, backed by the vast majority of the public, will go as many rounds as it takes to win that fight. So far, state efforts to defang, co-opt, or roll over opponents—in courts and at the ballot box—have been successful, largely because public support is so strong and policy has been carefully crafted with the backing of science and powerful public agencies.

Another way to counter opponents has been to welcome new business and industry with open arms and say goodbye to industries that can't keep up in the modern world. Advocates of climate and environmental efforts must keep their public policy goals sharply in mind and shape incentives to make them happen, not pander to outdated products and processes.

Efforts to counter climate change must engage all levels of public authority—state, local, federal, special districts, executive branch, legislative branch, and the judiciary. The climate actions needed are diverse, and authority for them is dispersed. For example, dozens of separate government departments and agencies at state and local levels have mandated roles to develop and enforce aspects of AB 32 and SB 32. All levels of government need to engage, work toward the same goals, and backstop one another. Different jurisdictions have control of various pollution sources. All factions need to advocate for the common good: protecting human health and the environment.

This book is a call to action. A long-term game plan or strategy is critical to leadership in climate efforts and policy. There are myriad specific areas to pursue: energy efficiency, clean cars, renewable energy, clean air and water, land-use planning, and saving forests are all necessary. And there are other important issues relevant to a particular city, state, or country.

Leaders must become expert on the topics, decide what success looks like, and determine how it can be measured if the policies are to be successfully implemented. Once they have a vision, they should promulgate it, starting by including their main points in every presentation, speech, conversation, essay, and op-ed commentary.

They must educate other influence makers and not be afraid to have them adopt, and even adapt, their views and speak up as though they own them. The effort might include turning to local universities, think tanks, government agencies, research firms, environmental organizations, and other respected intellectual and scientific figures to reinforce the policymakers' views and help describe policy paths to reach the goals.

Advocates for environmental policy can reach out through social media and to print and electronic news media as a resource to produce stories and editorials on the subject matter and results of research. They should make a good case for why this policy is important.

Policy solutions that can be achieved through good regulations or laws should be developed and shared with lawmakers and bureaucrats. When a new policy seems firmly on track, leaders can turn to a new element of action to address another contributor to climate change, and work to make that happen, too.

Now, more than ever, California is a model for climate change action across all jurisdictions—local, national, and international—and this book is a travel guide for those on the road to climate leadership. Visionary leaders—those willing to take a stand on energy and environmental policy over the long-term—can make a difference for many years. Multiplied across the globe, such leadership will change the world.

LA SKYLINE WITH CITY HALL, 2016
© Allen J. Schaben 2017, Los Angeles Times

Charts and Graphs

The *following tables and charts illustrate key trends and facts about the California economy and environment.*

\multicolumn{3}{CALIFORNIA'S WORLD RANKING 2015 GROSS DOMESTIC PRODUCT (In current US$)}

Rank	Countries	($billions)
1	**UNITED STATES**	$ 17,947
2	China	$ 10,983
3	Japan	$ 4,123
4	Germany	$ 3,358
5	United Kingdom	$ 2,849
6	**CALIFORNIA**	$ 2,459
7	France	$ 2,422
8	India	$ 2,091
9	Italy	$ 1,816
10	Brazil	$ 1,773
11	Canada	$ 1,552
12	Korea	$ 1,377
13	Russia	$ 1,325
14	Australia	$ 1,224
15	Spain	$ 1,200
16	Mexico	$ 1,144
17	Indonesia	$ 859
18	Netherlands	$ 738
19	Turkey	$ 734
20	Switzerland	$ 665

Source: International Monetary Fund, World Economic Outlook Database

TOTAL GHG EMISSIONS FROM ENERGY CONSUMPTION RANKING
TOTAL EMISSIONS IN 2013

RANK	REGION	MILLION MTCO$_2$e
1	CHINA	8686.9
2	UNITED STATES	5401.7
3	EU-28	3759.7
4	INDIA	1886.5
5	RUSSIA	1726.3
6	JAPAN	1257.1
7	GERMANY	805.0
8	SOUTH KOREA	651.0
9	IRAN	611.8
10	SAUDI ARABIA	593.6
11	CANADA	564.3
12	BRAZIL	534.5
13	UNITED KINGDOM	488.0
14	SOUTH AFRICA	481.9
15	MEXICO	455.3
16	INDONESIA	442.4
17	AUSTRALIA	385.2
18	FRANCE	366.5
19	ITALY	362.2
20	CALIFORNIA	353.1
21	POLAND	321.5
22	TURKEY	318.7
23	THAILAND	300.7
24	TAIWAN	294.9
25	UKRAINE	291.1

Source: Next 10

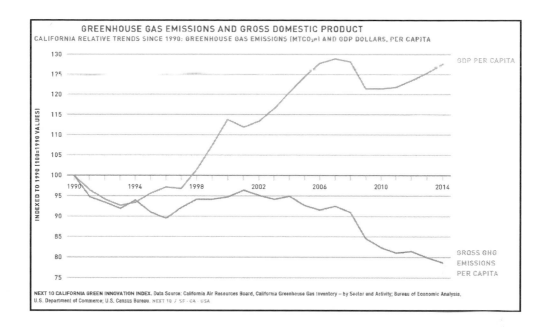

GREENHOUSE GAS EMISSIONS AND GROSS DOMESTIC PRODUCT
CALIFORNIA RELATIVE TRENDS SINCE 1990: GREENHOUSE GAS EMISSIONS (MTCO$_2$e) AND GDP DOLLARS, PER CAPITA

GDP PER CAPITA

GROSS GHG EMISSIONS PER CAPITA

INDEXED TO 1990 (100=1990 VALUES)

NEXT 10 CALIFORNIA GREEN INNOVATION INDEX. Data Source: California Air Resources Board, California Greenhouse Gas Inventory – by Sector and Activity; Bureau of Economic Analysis, U.S. Department of Commerce; U.S. Census Bureau. NEXT 10 / SF · CA · USA

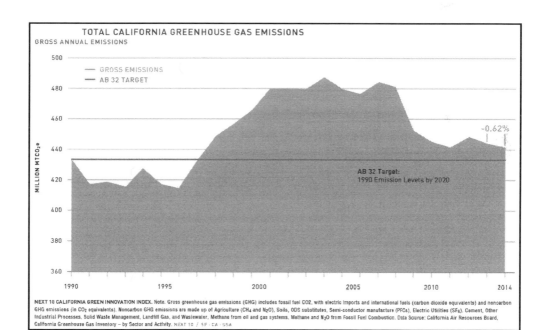

TOTAL CALIFORNIA GREENHOUSE GAS EMISSIONS
GROSS ANNUAL EMISSIONS

GROSS EMISSIONS
AB 32 TARGET

MILLION MTCO$_2$e

-0.62%

AB 32 Target:
1990 Emission Levels by 2020

NEXT 10 CALIFORNIA GREEN INNOVATION INDEX. Note. Gross greenhouse gas emissions (GHG) includes fossil fuel CO2, with electric imports and international fuels (carbon dioxide equivalents) and noncarbon GHG emissions (in CO$_2$ equivalents). Noncarbon GHG emissions are made up of Agriculture (CH$_4$ and N$_2$O), Soils, ODS substitutes, Semi-conductor manufacture (PFCs), Electric Utilities (SF$_6$). Cement, Other Industrial Processes, Solid Waste Management, Landfill Gas, and Wastewater, Methane from oil and gas systems, Methane and N$_2$O from Fossil Fuel Combustion. Data Source: California Air Resources Board, California Greenhouse Gas Inventory – by Sector and Activity. NEXT 10 / SF · CA · USA

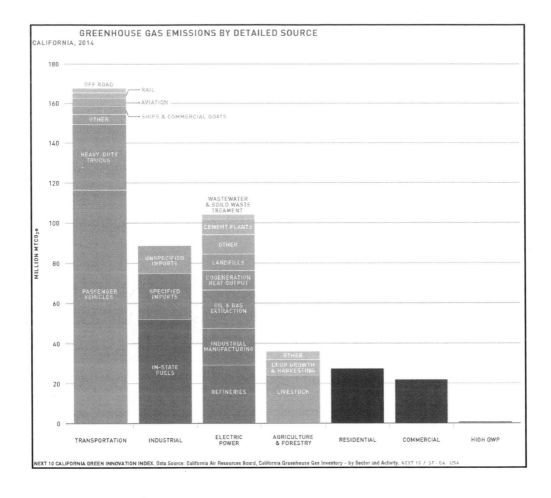

GREENHOUSE GAS EMISSIONS BY DETAILED SOURCE
CALIFORNIA, 2014

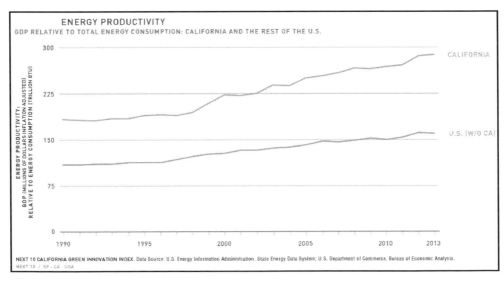

ENERGY PRODUCTIVITY
GDP RELATIVE TO TOTAL ENERGY CONSUMPTION: CALIFORNIA AND THE REST OF THE U.S.

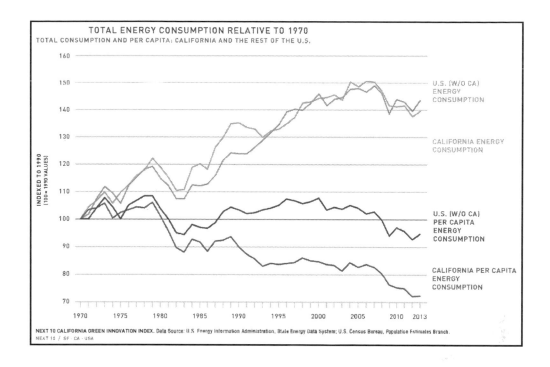

TOTAL ENERGY CONSUMPTION RELATIVE TO 1970
TOTAL CONSUMPTION AND PER CAPITA: CALIFORNIA AND THE REST OF THE U.S.

U.S. (W/O CA) ENERGY CONSUMPTION

CALIFORNIA ENERGY CONSUMPTION

U.S. (W/O CA) PER CAPITA ENERGY CONSUMPTION

CALIFORNIA PER CAPITA ENERGY CONSUMPTION

NEXT 10 CALIFORNIA GREEN INNOVATION INDEX. Data Source: U.S. Energy Information Administration, State Energy Data System; U.S. Census Bureau, Population Estimates Branch.
NEXT 10 / SF · CA · USA

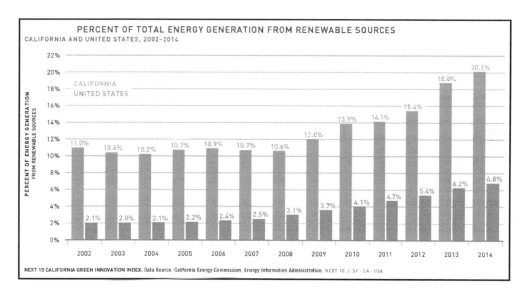

PERCENT OF TOTAL ENERGY GENERATION FROM RENEWABLE SOURCES
CALIFORNIA AND UNITED STATES, 2002–2014

CALIFORNIA
UNITED STATES

NEXT 10 CALIFORNIA GREEN INNOVATION INDEX. Data Source: California Energy Commission, Energy Information Administration. NEXT 10 / SF · CA · USA

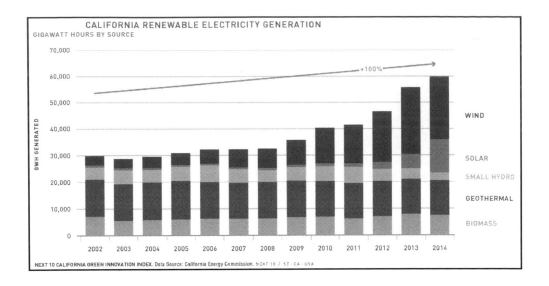

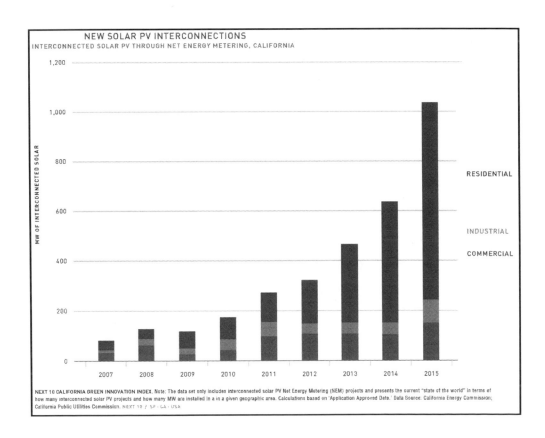

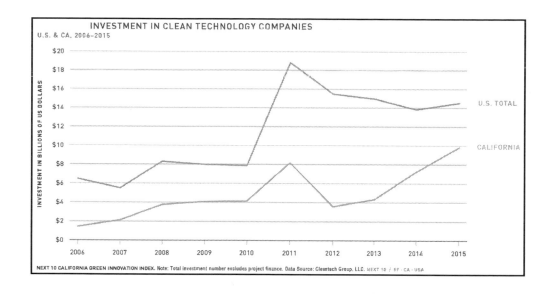

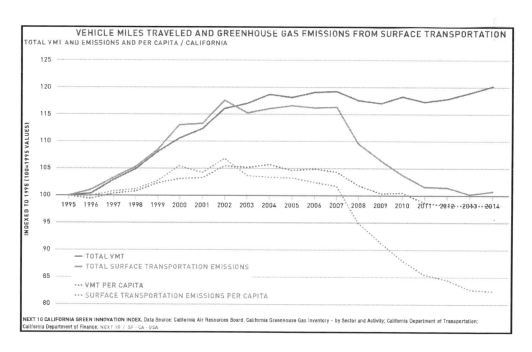

ELECTRICITY PRICES AND BILLS (INFLATION-ADJUSTED)					
	RESIDENTIAL	PRICE PER kWh	AVERAGE MONTHLY BILL		
		2014	2004	2014	10 YEAR % CHANGE
	CALIFORNIA	$0.16	$86.54	$91.26	5.5%
	FLORIDA	$0.12	$133.59	$129.86	-2.8%
	ILLINOIS	$0.12	$77.21	$88.78	15.0%
	NEW YORK	$0.20	$105.90	$118.63	12.0%
	OHIO	$0.13	$91.93	$112.62	22.5%
	PENNSYLVANIA	$0.13	$98.94	$113.72	14.9%
	TEXAS	$0.12	$142.78	$137.39	-3.8%
	UNITED STATES	$0.13	$101.63	$114.09	12.3%

APPROPRIATIONS FOR CALIFORNIA CLIMATE INVESTMENTS FY 2013–14 THROUGH 2015–16	
PROGRAM	APPROPRIATIONS TOTAL ($M)
HIGH SPEED RAIL PROJECT	$850
TRANSIT AND INTERCITY RAIL CAPITAL PROGRAM	$265
LOW CARBON TRANSIT OPERATIONS PROGRAM	$145
AFFORDABLE HOUSING AND SUSTAINABLE COMMUNITIES	$610
LOW CARBON TRANSPORTATION	$325
LOW-INCOME WEATHERIZATION PROGRAM	$154
ENERGY EFFICIENCY FOR PUBLIC BUILDINGS	$20
CLIMATE SMART AGRICULTURE	$75
WATER ENERGY EFFICIENCY	$70
WETLANDS AND WATERSHED RESTORATION	$27
SUSTAINABLE FORESTS	$42
WASTE DIVERSION	$31
TOTAL APPROPRIATIONS	$2,614

Acknowledgements

This book was made possible in part by a grant from the nonprofit Energy Foundation. Vice President of Policy, Dan Adler, offered thoughtful observations that helped shape our thinking. Mary Nichols, chair, California Air Resources Board and J.R. DeShazo, chair, Luskin Center for Innovation, UCLA gave us our earliest encouragement and guidance. Many others contributed their time and knowledge via personal interviews and email exchanges. In no particular order, they include: Robert Foster, former mayor, Long Beach, and retired president, Southern California Edison Company; Vikram Budhraja, president, Electric Power Group; Susan Kennedy, CEO of Advanced Microgrid, former PUC Commissioner, and chief of staff to Governor Arnold Schwarzenegger; Arthur Rosenfeld, physicist and former California Energy Commissioner; Daniel Kammen, professor of energy and resources, UC Berkeley; Fabian Núñez, former speaker of the California State Assembly; Fran Pavley, retired California state senator; Ralph Cavanagh, co-director of the Natural Resources Defense Fund energy program; Terry Tamminen, CEO of the Leonardo Di Caprio Foundation; Bonnie Reiss, global director, Schwarzenegger Institute for State and Global Policy, University of Southern California; Robert Weisenmiller, chairman, California Energy Commission; Dr. Dan Sperling, CARB board member and founding director of the Institute of Transportation Studies, U.C. Davis; Craig Ebert, president, Climate Action Reserve; Gary Gero, the Reserve's former president; and Wendy James, president of the Better World Group.

From the California Public Utilities Commission: Michael Picker, president; Molly Sterkel, Energy Division; Edward Randolph, chief, Energy Division; Julie Fitch, administrative law judge; and Carol Brown, retired former chief of staff to the president. Also, David Freeman, author, energy expert, and retired head of the Los Angeles Department of Water and Power; Lynn Schenk, former chief of staff to Governor Gray Davis; and Daniel Mazmanian, professor, Schwarzenegger Institute for State and Global Policy were helpful.

We also thank Joshua Bar-Lev, former senior officer, BrightSource Energy; John Woolard, former CEO, BrightSource Energy; Kevin de León, president *pro tem*, California state Senate; Richard Maullin, chairman, California Independent System Operator (CAISO); Sunne McPeak, president, California Emerging Technology Fund; Lyndon Rive, CEO, SolarCity; Jan Smutny-Jones, president, California Independent Energy Producers; Charles Winner, principal, Winner & Associates; and Mason Willrich, former chair of the CAISO and energy entrepreneur.

Special thanks goes to Next 10 and its *California Green Innovation Index*. All the charts and tables in the book come from that nonprofit organization.

Excellent counsel throughout, especially on structure and coherence, was given by Narda Zacchino, author of *California Comeback: How a "Failed State" Became a Model for the Nation*, and executive editor of Heyday publications. Research assistant Helen Wang and project manager Jennifer Reza made critical contributions.

Unlimited amounts of patience were provided by the authors' spouses, retired state Senator Carol J. Liu, and retired Superior Court Judge David Minning. We are indebted to many others and thank everyone who helped and encouraged us along the way, believing that this was a book that should be written.

Glossary

AB Assembly Bill, a bill authored by a member of the California State Assembly.

AES A large independent power company.

ARB (also **CARB**) California Air Resources Board. The state agency responsible for clean air and combating climate change. It is also the only state agency in the United States that can also set vehicle emission standards.

BrightSource Oakland based solar energy company, successor to Luz Solar and builder of one of the world's largest solar generating facilities at Ivanpah, California.

CalEPA California Environmental Protection Agency. The California Air Resources Board (ARB/CARB) is part of CalEPA.

California Solar Initiative Effort led by the PUC and CEC to incentivize and support the installation of 1 million residential and business rooftop solar collectors to generate electricity.

CCEEB California Council for Environmental and Economic Balance, founded in 1973 by unions, businesses, utilities and community leaders.

CAISO see ISO.

CEC California Energy Commission. The CEC is responsible for statewide energy policy and planning. It sets efficiency standards, sites new power plants and conducts energy research.

CEQA California Environmental Quality Act, enacted in 1969, which requires an environmental impact analysis of almost all development and building projects in the state.

Coastal Commission (Also California Coastal Commission) The state agency charged with preserving and enhancing the entire California coastline.

Conservation Strategy Group A consulting firm headquartered in Sacramento, California.

DG Distributed Generation. DG provides small amounts of electrical power, such as rooftop solar. This is distinguished from a large power plant.

Duke Power A large independent electric power producer.

EAP Energy Action Plan Prioritizes and guides energy policy, planning and execution in California.

EDF Environmental Defense Fund, a national environmental organization.

EPA The federal Environmental Protection Agency, headquartered in Washington, DC.

FERC Federal Energy Regulatory Commission, headquartered in Washington, DC, with jurisdiction over aspects of California energy.

GHGs Greenhouse gases. These various atmospheric gases produce a "greenhouse effect," warming the climate.

ISO Also **CAISO**. California Independent System Operator, which runs and coordinates the high voltage electrical system in California.

Loading Order The prioritization of electric resources for California.

Mirant A large independent electric power producer.

NEM Net Energy Metering, the method by which excess rooftop-generated solar energy is sold to a utility by a resident or business at a price set by the PUC.

NGO Non-Governmental Organization, such as a consumer or environmental group not funded by government agencies, e.g., Environmental Defense Fund.

NHTSA National Highway Traffic Safety Administration, headquartered in Washington, DC. It sets national miles per gallon efficiency standards for cars and trucks.

NRDC Natural Resources Defense Council, an NGO and environmental organization.

NRG A large independent electric power producer.

Parabolic Trough A portion of a solar collector used to gather and generate electricity.

PEV Collaborative Plug In Vehicle organization supporting electric vehicles.

PG&E Pacific Gas and Electric Company, a San Francisco based utility.

PUC California Public Utilities Commission. The PUC regulates privately owned electric and gas utilities, such as PG&E, Southern California Edison and San Diego Gas and Electric. The PUC also regulates other types of companies, such as telecommunications, transportation and water.

R20 A worldwide voluntary city, state, region and sub-national organization created to combat climate change, led in significant part by former governor Arnold Schwarzenegger.

SB Senate Bill, a bill authored by a member of the California State Senate.

SDG&E San Diego Gas and Electric Company, a San Diego based utility, part of Sempra Energy.

SCE Southern California Edison, a Rosemead based electric utility, part of Edison International.

Sleeving Purchasing power on behalf of a credit-weak entity, e.g., the State Department of Water Resources buying power for credit-impaired utilities during the energy crisis.

Under2MOU A worldwide voluntary city, state, region and sub-national organization created to combat climate change, led in significant part by Governor Edmund G. Brown, Jr.

APPENDIXES

APPENDIX I

Progress Report on California Electricity Solutions

**Submitted to
Governor Gray Davis**

By
Michael R. Peevey
S. David Freeman
Vikram S. Budhraja

Advisers to the Governor

March 2, 2001

Progress Report on California Electricity Solutions

Section I
Power Purchase Portfolio Plan and Recommendations
Goal

Create a portfolio of power contracts for the "net-short" needs (1/3 of total) to provide price stability and predictability and reduce reliance on spot market.

Strategy

- Build a power purchase portfolio to provide power to California consisting of contracts that cover power supplies for different time periods
  - Less than 90 days
  - 3 years
  - 5 years
  - 10 years
- Give priorities to contracts that result in construction of new power plants and offer long-term price stability.
- Limit 10-year contracts to entities that can provide power supplies starting no later than third quarter 2001.
- Contract with a diverse mix of suppliers and power companies.
- Provide for up to 50% of needs for 2005-10 period through long-term contracts. Portfolio to consist of base load, dispatchable, peaking, unit contingent, and other building blocks. Balance to be acquired from the market including spot market in out years when a surplus is expected.

Status

Resources to start negotiations with power suppliers were mobilized during the last week of January. The team has been led by David Freeman and Vikram Budhraja with contracts, legal, technical, and analytic support provided by Department of Water Resources (DWR) and its consultants. The negotiations were conducted in February 2001 out of the Governor's Office in Los Angeles. Over approximately 20 days, in-person and telephone meetings and negotiations were conducted with all major suppliers, including Calpine, Williams, Duke, Mirant, Dynegy, PacifiCorp, BPA, Reliant,

Powerex, Constellation, El Paso, Morgan Stanley, Sempra, PG&E's National Energy Group, Edison Mission Energy, Enron, AES, DWP, Alliance, Merrill Lynch, Goldman Sachs, and others.

———

This has been a major effort and we have reached agreement on commercial terms with all of the above named companies except two. The DWR team deserves much credit for assisting us in a successful effort that is by far the largest concentrated cost-effective procurement of electricity ever undertaken. Forty agreements are in place. The maximum megawatts under contracts in any one-year exceeds 10,500 MW. Approximately 5,000 MW of these supplies will be from new power plants targeted to come on-line in the next 24 months. These are complex contracts and negotiations. In the normal course of business each contract can take several months to finalize all terms. The price, quantity, and term have been agreed upon with all these suppliers and contracts are either signed or in legal review to finalize detailed terms and conditions.

These contracts and agreements have resulted in:

- Increased DWR forward purchases by the end of February to 75% in the day-ahead and 95% in the day- and hour-ahead markets, substantially reducing dependence on the real-time market;
- Reduced DWR average cost of purchases from $330/MWh in the spot market to portfolio averaging $228/MWh by the end of February;
- A diversified long-term portfolio of contracts that meets the goal of committing up to 50% of the unmet needs. The average portfolio price of $79/MWh for the first five years and $61/MWh for the second five years;
- Expediting construction of new power plants with 5,000 MW slated to come on-line within 24 months including some as early as this summer.

These agreements include seasonal power exchanges with Bonneville Power Administration (BPA) and Powerex, which offer significant operational benefits and reduce dependence on the spot market.

Long-term agreements have been reached for a significant portfolio of power purchases

	2001	2002	2003	2004	2005	2006-10
Total #	30	31	29	27	24	19
Total MW	5,582	7,769	9,671	10,642	8,992	8,742
Average Price $/MWh	105	91	79	73	68	61

Recommendation on Managing Power Purchases

Managing the power purchase portfolio is a **MAJOR** undertaking and cannot be done over time with current State resources. The capabilities for power portfolio management reside with utilities, consultants, and power traders. The State should name a "power portfolio czar" for managing the power purchases for a period of no more than two years and with negotiating authority and ability to contract for the necessary expertise. The State should plan to turn the function back to utilities as soon as practical.

Section II
State Energy Reorganization – Review and Recommendations

In considering where to place the new activities the State is undertaking for at least a number of years, it is useful to survey the existing organizations. California is "blessed" with quite a number – they are:

	# of Board Members	# of Employees
(1) California Public Utilities Commission (PUC)	5	900
(2) California Energy Commission (CEC)	5	450
(3) Independent System Operator (ISO)	5	700
(4) California Power Exchange (CalPX)	30	200
(5) Electricity Oversight Board (EOB)	5	18
(6) Department of Water Resources (DWR)	None	2,900

The functions can be broken down into four categories:

1 – Regulatory
2 – Planning
3 – Siting
4 – Operational

The new activities requiring State involvement are the purchasing of electricity, which is now underway, ownership and expansion of the transmission system, expediting power plant construction, possibly a role in financing new power plants, and investments in conservation and load management.

In addition, the large increases in the cost of natural gas and infrastructure bottlenecks in transportation and storage also require State attention. The runaway price of natural gas is a major cause of sky-high electric prices. The State must have an agency that takes responsibility for addressing this issue.

In considering where to place these activities, it is important to note that the State has too many energy agencies. They duplicate each other causing confusion as to the State's policy. Proposals for transmission projects or power plants made by investor-owned utilities have been rejected for nearly 15 years and approvals for construction of power plants by independent power companies have been slow in coming. The Governor is required to name a total of two-dozen people to head various existing agencies, with no clear focus and considerable waste of money. And, there is no one really responsible for "keeping the lights on at reasonable price," or speaking with one voice at FERC.

As to the home for the new activities the State is undertaking, the CPUC is a regulatory agency and clearly not the appropriate agency. The CEC does not have the leadership or the culture fro prompt action and operational experience. As to the ISO, PX, or EOB, they are obviously not the place for major new operating activities.

It is quite clear that the existing "alphabet soup" of agencies in the energy field needs to be streamlined. The PX is in the process of dying. The ISO could be transferred intact to a new agency. The EOB is not needed and it should be abolished. The CEC power plant siting functions could be transferred to the PUC, and its other functions of planning, research, and conservation and load management could easily be put in the new agency.

It is important to point out the CPUC as currently structured and operating is dysfunctional and requires substantial overhaul to make it responsive to meeting State energy policy needs. State's current shortages in power supplies, transmission bottlenecks, gas pipeline bottlenecks, lack of in-state gas storage can to a large part be traced to CPUC decisions over the last 15-20 years. CPUC must be altered in terms of its focus, leadership, staffing, and size.

The State needs to create a new agency to handle the new responsibilities. The options for housing the new agency are:

1. Add the responsibilities to DWR;
2. Create a new agency;
3. Consolidate all of the electricity agencies into two (2) agencies – one for the regulation and one for planning and operations.

Adding power purchases, the construction of power plants and operation of the transmission system to DWR has surface appeal. DWR has operational experience: it is a place where power purchases are taking place and it does have real world experience in the power sector through operation of the power plants associated with the State Water Project.

However, without a strong infusion of outside talent that is **in charge**. DWR cannot really handle the new functions. It is very difficult to attract good people unless they are given permanent employment and the authority to get the job done. And while the Governor can empower some outsiders during an emergency, the idea of DWR taking on these new tasks can work only if there is in effect a new agency within the DWR umbrella that has independent authority and the ability to recruit people outside the civil service system. Hence, the conclusion that a "new agency" is needed no matter where it is located.

The package of activities the State is undertaking – power purchases, transmission system, possibly power plant construction, conservation and load management investment, and gas infrastructure investments are fundamentally different than the work of the existing energy agencies, and much broader than DWR's scope of activities. Even in the area of power purchases, DWR would have to "build" power trading and power portfolio management skills found in utilities and power companies.

To attract the kind of talent needed, an organization structured with responsibility of government, but with all the flexibility and freedom to act quickly, hire and fire outside the civil services, and provide financial incentives like a private company is needed. The ISO organization model of a non-profit outfit that is NOT a State agency seems attractive. The new agency should likewise be set up as a non-profit public benefit corporation with a small Board chosen by the Governor and a strong CEO as the head.

The new agency with a dynamic chief executive would be most likely to recruit the kind of people that will make it a success. Trying to place the "new agency" beneath an existing State agency would make it more difficult to achieve the flexibility it needs or attract the talent necessary to discharge its responsibilities.

Planning to achieve a surplus and reasonable prices as well as the development of energy policy needs to be focused in one place, even when this emergency is over. One of the current problems is the "competition" between the PUC and CEC, which put out competing projections and differing policies complicated even further by the activities of the EOB.

The new action-oriented agency should be required to report annually firm projections of the State's total power requirements for maintaining a surplus. If private enterprises do not actually build enough capacity it will be the builder of last resort or see that others do so in a timely fashion through execution of power purchase contracts and or financing. Power purchasing activities now placed in DWR would fit nicely with the new agency role of "keeping the lights on."

Therefore, it is recommended that the State end up with two agencies instead of five or six; namely, the PUC (refocused and streamlined) and the new action-oriented agency, that will include the new duties, the present functions of the ISO, and the planning, research, and conservation functions of the CEC.

The subject of air quality must be considered because unless there is a harmony between air quality and the energy agencies, there will continue to be controversy and delays rather than power plants completed on time. The Governor, by executive Order, should create an energy policy council that would include the head of CARB, head of this new agency, head of CPUC, with the Governor's Chief of Staff as Chair. It should be empowered to harmonize the programs of various agencies to achieve the desired result consistent with maintaining basic environmental standards.

Summary Recommendation for Energy Reorganization

Create a new non-profit public benefit corporation to oversee the functions of:

- Transmission Planning and Operations
- Power Purchases
- Energy Planning and Research
- Conservation and Load Management
- Gas Supply and Infrastructure

The new energy corporation should have a five person Board of Directors chosen by the Governor. The agency should be run by a

Chief Executive Officer. The current ISO should be subsumed within the new agency and become responsible for transmission planning and operations. The power purchasing function should be transitioned back to the utilities as soon as possible within the next two years. In the interim, the agency could oversee the power purchase function but rely on DWR to handle it with support from consultants. The new energy corporation should be responsible for statewide energy planning, research, conservation and load management programs.

Section III
Transition Plan
The transition from the current structure to setting up the new energy corporation will require 3-to-6 months at a minimum. The State is faced with critical energy decisions to address the current emergency situation and cannot afford to lose the momentum resulting from State actions on power purchases, expediting power plant construction, utility negotiations, and other initiatives under discussion. The bureaucracy needs a "czar or two" with unqualified support of the Governor to maintain the momentum of the last few months and get the new energy corporation off the ground. This requires someone with the requisite expertise that can take on this challenge on a full-time basis. To allow for such a transition and until the new energy corporation is up and running, the Governors Energy Advisers, namely Michael Peevey, David Freeman, and Vikram Budhraja could be tasked on a part-time occasional basis to act as Interim Board and provide advice and oversee the implementation of state Energy Initiatives.

Section IV
Actions Needed

1. Executive Order – Conservation and Demand Management
2. Transmission Action Plan
3. California's High Gas Prices and Recommended Actions
4. Executive Order – Hydro Electric Resources

5. Distributed Generation
6. ISO Streamlining
7. Comprehensive Statewide Electricity Action Plan Checklist

Executive order – Conservation and Demand Management

California has a unique opportunity for the summer of 2001 to achieve significant cost savings and greater reliability by conserving energy and reducing demand on a large-scale basis. The short-term wholesale cost of electricity is so high that the State can save money by paying consumers for conservation and demand reduction. Instead of "buying" electricity, the State could "buy" conservation and demand reduction from consumers, creating a simple, market oriented approach that rewards consumers and saves money for the State.

This could be done by issuing an Executive Order on Conservation and Demand Management:

"To encourage efficient use of energy resources and achieve at least an overall 10% reduction in energy demand, California utilities are ordered to implement a market-based voluntary conservation and demand management program. Under this program, the State Power Fund will pay each and every customer that achieves at least a 20% reduction in their consumption an amount equal to a savings that they have achieved. Thus, if June to September consumption during 2000 was 4,000 kwh and it is reduced to below 3,200 kwh during the same period in 2001, consumers will get rewarded twice- once through their bill savings and secondly through a payment from the State, thereby creating a market oriented incentive for consumers to conserve. For customers with TOU meters, consumption reduction will be measured during the June-September summer peak period of noon to 6 p.m."

The State would rather pay citizens the existing retail rate for saving electricity rather than pay higher prices to generators for purchase of electricity during critical summer periods. Such a program will prevent brownouts, reduce wholesale prices, reduce emissions, and overcome supply shortages. State will benefit from substantial purchase power savings, which will exceed payments for conservation and demand management.

Transmission Action Plan

The high voltage transmission grid is the electrical highway for transporting electricity from power plants to consumers. Investments in California's grid have lagged the growth in the economy. The cost of the transmission grid is less than 10% of the total cost of electricity. However, deficiencies and lack of investment can cost billions of dollars in the wholesale market, as has been the case in California. Steps that should be taken to enhance the transmission grid and reduce overall costs to Californians include:

1. Optimize Use of Existing transmission Assets.
    *   Under emergency action by the Governor require all utilities to have rights to transmission, including investor-owned utilities, federal power agencies, and municipal utilities to release their unused transmission to the ISO in the day-ahead market as opposed to holding on to it until real-time.

    To implement this action we recommend the following Executive Order.

    "To optimize the use of California's high voltage transmission grid during the period of electrical emergency, a Transmission Task Force will be established under the Chairmanship of Michael Kahn. Task Force members will include representatives from Independent System Operator, California Department of Water Resources, Pacific Gas and Electric, Southern California Edison, San Diego Gas and Electric, and California Municipal Utilities Association. The Transmission Task Force shall implement coordinated transmission dispatch that maximizes use of scarce transmission resources during the period of electrical emergency. Such coordinated dispatch shall be implemented within two weeks."

2. Strengthen the transmission grid by urgent action to de-bottleneck and build new transmission. Funding should be included in pending legislation to pay for transmission upgrades.
    *   Path 15
        a. Implement remedial action scheme to provide 100-200 MW
        b. Upgrade the 230 kV transmission system and add new transformers at a cost of $10-20 Million to add 400-500 MW.

    c. Build the new 500 kV Los Banos-Gates at a cost of $250-300 Million on an expedited basis.

- Valley-Rainbow 500 kV line to relieve import constraints into San Diego area.
- New transmission line and substation into the San Francisco area (the City of San Francisco and others continue to oppose new lines to the peninsula or new generation on the peninsula, but one or the other is needed.)
- New transmission line and substation into Fresno to prevent voltage collapse. PG&E proposed the Gates-Gregg 500 kV line for this need, but the line was rejected by the CPUC; a Gates-Gregg line in combination with a Gregg-Los Banos line could be an alternate to the Los Banos-Gates line solution to Path 15, and solve both problems).
- Upgrading the Palo Verde-North Gila-Imperial Valley-Miguel line with higher rated series capacitors to relieve congestion between Arizona and southern California.

3. Streamline Need Determination

Approve construction of transmission lines after ISO has made the determination for need without requiring a separate CPCN or requiring a separate assessment of alternatives to transmission.

4. Transmission Upgrades Beyond The First Point of Interconnection

Assign cost responsibility and make funding available to utilities to invest in an upgrade transmission grid beyond the first point of interconnection and assure a full cost recovery for such upgrades. This is essential to assure interconnection of new generation on an expedited basis.

5. Request FERC to suspend existing transmission queuing rules to expedite interconnection of new generation based on in-service dates, as opposed to when the initial application was made.

Transmission actions are as vital as new power plants and conservation, if reasonable price and reliability is to be achieved. Every day of delay means another day of possible shortages and high prices.

California High Gas Prices and Recommended Actions

Californians have been hit by high prices for natural gas to heat their homes, run their business and produce electricity. What went wrong? Where is the problem? And most importantly, how do we fix it?

In the early part of the year 2000, natural gas prices increased perhaps as much as 50% above the 1999 levels. While this was alarming, energy experts had rational explanations. Strong demand from a robust economy; supply stagnation from an indifferent energy industry; the weather; hurricane season; high Internet induced electric use; temporary pipeline disruptions; the low inventory of natural gas in storage; the weather again.

- In July 1999, Californians could buy natural gas at the trading hub in San Juan, New Mexico for about $2.25/MMBtu, and have it transported for another $0.25/MMBtu. So for about $2.50/MMBtu they could get the natural gas into California and produce electricity for between 3 and 5 cents per kilowatt-hour.
- In July 2000, the gas in San Juan was about $3.60/MMBtu but the California border price had risen to $4.60/MMBtu, an increase of 400 percent. But the momentum was unrelenting. By the third week in November 2000, natural gas reached $6.25 and transportation $17.00 into southern California. The blowout continued to a climax on December 12, 2000 when natural gas at the wellhead rose to about $10.00 and California's 25-cent transportation costs had exploded to an astounding $50.00 in the spot market.

While prices have settled somewhat since then, probably just a lull in the storm, we are seeing natural gas transportation – basin to California border – remaining in the nosebleed regions of $10/MMBtu or 20-30 times its rational value, threatening to trash the world's sixth largest economy.

The salient feature on this frightening landscape is the experiment the FERC began by issuing its Order 637, on February 9, 2000, which removed the cap on the price that could be charged for short-term natural gas pipeline capacity. This allowed the price for gas transportation to rise, or skyrocket, to whatever heights the market or marketers could contrive. Without proper government regulation, a transportation service capped at no more than 30 cents, providing its owners a reasonable rate of return, had mutated into a $50 monster threatening to devour not only California's economy, but also numerous economies in the United States and elsewhere.

The appropriate fix would be to restore federal regulation of interstate pipelines based on cost-of-service principles, which have worked well for decades and cap gas transportation rates to their pre-Order 637 levels. In issuing its Order, the FERC suggested that a two-year trial period would be necessary to determine if removal of the cap on interstate gas transportation rates were a good idea or not. The evidence is convincing enough after 12 months to call a halt to this experiment. California has been rendered a deep wound, which doesn't need to bleed anymore to prove itself fatal.

Recommendations – Reducing Gas Costs

Critical to reducing electricity prices is access to reasonably priced gas. Gas currently accounts for 80-90% of the spot market price of electricity.

The State needs to reduce gas costs by:

- Encouraging development of new gas pipeline capacity to California.
- Requiring California gas utilities to debottleneck in State gas distribution infrastructure.
- Building additional gas storage capacity and adding to gas storage reserves to dampen out price volatility.
- Acquiring gas transportation capacity during next "open season" by El Paso and other pipelines.
- Encouraging FERC to renew regulation and pricing of interstate gas pipelines.
- Assigning responsibility to the new energy agency to acquire gas resources if market prices continue to be sky high.

Executive Order – Hydro Electric Resources

to optimize use of statewide hydro resources to meet the electric power needs of the citizens of California, the California Department of

Water Resources (CDWR) is directed to establish a Hydro Operations Task Force comprising of representatives of CDWR, Independent System Operator, Pacific Gas and Electric, and Southern California Edison. They Hydro Operations Task Force will be chaired by Richard Ferreira and implement a statewide hydro resource dispatch within two weeks.

Promote Distributed Generation (DG)

Overcoming the shortage of electric power plants and transmission capacity requires the utilization of every available option. That means that distributed generation – namely fuel cells, micro turbines, and solar panels (photovoltaic cells) need to be promoted and installed.

The major impediment to large-scale deployment of DG is the imposition of standby charges by utilities and their tendency to be slow and expensive in interconnecting these small-scale power sources.

We, therefore, recommend that the PUC, at once, eliminate standby charges and order streamlined, cost-based interconnection policies by the distribution utilities in California.

Distributed generation, which ranges from 30 kW to 1 or 2 MW generators can in the next few years add hundreds of megawatts of power located near loads that will add to the reliability and adequacy of our power supply. It needs to be encouraged.

In addition, there are several thousand megawatts of standby generation that could be mobilized during critical shortage periods. We recommend that the utilities should immediately undertake a program to install the necessary equipment to activate standby generation to help during emergencies.

ISO Streamlining

There are several actions that should be taken to improve and focus ISO operations and reduce costs, as outlined below:

1. Pay as Bid for ancillary services and energy.
2. ISO directed dispatch to relieve transmission congestion and optimize usage.
3. Transition ISO to real-time purchases of 5% or less through coordinated hydro dispatch and use of peakers.

4. Limit ISO to transmission planning, real-time dispatch, ancillary services, reliability management, energy scheduling, and management of transmission grid.
5. Procurement of generation in forward markets (peaking, long-term contracts, day-ahead) should not be done by ISO.
6. Customer conservation, demand management, standby generation, distributed generation programs, etc., should not be handled by ISO.
7. Dispatch of peak shaving and emergency resources – peakers, demand management, hydro, standby generation should be handled by ISO in coordination with DWR and utilities.
8. Implement ISO generator unit outage coordination and availability standards.
9. Stabilize ISO operations with a forward portfolio, outage coordination, coordinated hydro dispatch, and coordinated transmission dispatch. Hold off on other operating and market reforms.

Comprehensive Statewide
Electircity Action Plan Checklist
A checklist of Statewide Action Items to address California's Electric Emergency that have been discussed in this report, are enumerated below.

1. Purchase under term contracts and reduce dependence on spot market.
2. Expedite construction of peaking capacity and new power plants.
3. Remove transmission bottlenecks and promote new transmission construction
   - Path 15 ($250-350 Million)
   - Path 26 (Midway-Vincent)
   - Palo Verde Imports (PV-Miguel, Upgrade Capacity Bank)
4. Install Time-of-Use meters and implement rates to provide price signals to customers and promote price responsive energy management.
5. Implement aggressive conservation and load management program.

6. Activate standby generation for emergency use.
7. Implement market-based interruptible and demand reduction program.
8. Promote distributed generation – eliminate standby rates and implement net metering.
9. Coordinate dispatch of statewide hydro resources to optimize their use (ISO-DWR-SCE-PG&E).
10. Establish ISO generator unit outage coordination and availability standards.
11. Expedite environmental retrofit schedule for SCR and emission abatement equipment on existing gas-fired power plants.
12. Pursue upgrade of DC Intertie Terminal at Celilo through Bonneville Power Administration.
13. Streamline generation interconnections and transmission upgrade process for new generating power plants.
14. Establish NO_x emission fees for power generation (modify RECLAIM).
15. Maximize QF production.
16. Expedite new power plant licensing.
17. Expand in-state gas storage capacity (similar to Strategic Petroleum Reserve)

Summary Results of Power Purchase Activities

- Short-Term Power Agreements
- Contract Prices
- Long-Term Power Agreements 2001-2010
- Power Purchase Agreements - MW

Short-Term Power Agreements
As of March 1, 2001

Company	Start	Term	Product	MW
MIECO	2/15/2001	Bal. Feb	Peak	25
CFE	2/15/2001	Bal. Feb	Base	50
LADWP	2/15/2001	Thru April	Base	545
Sempra	2/15/2001	week	Base	5
Dynegy	2/16/2001	Thru Mar.	Peak	1,000
El Paso	2/17/2001	Bal. Feb	Peak	50
BP Energy	2/17/2001	Bal. Feb	Peak	50
PX BFM-Duke	2/19/2001	Bal. Feb	Peak	275
PX BFM-Duke	2/19/2001	Bal. Feb	Peak	300
Reliant	2/21/2001	30 days	Peak	316
Reliant	2/21/2001	30 days	Excess	3,468
Total MW				6,084
Total Agreements				11
Average Contract Price				$229
Price Reduction compared to spot market				27%

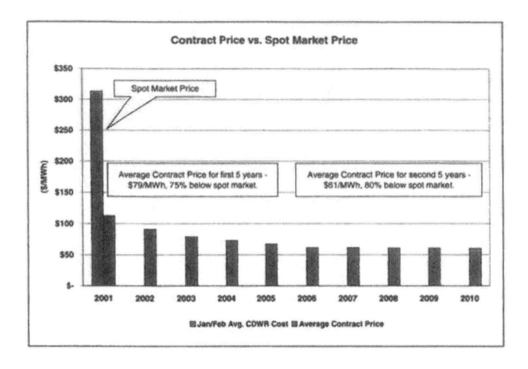

Long-Term Power Agreements 2001-2010
As of March 1, 2001

Company	Start	Term	Product	MW
El Paso	2/9/2001	5 yr	Peak	50
El Paso	2/9/2001	5 yr	Peak	50
BPA	2/13/2001	14 mos	Base	18
Morgan Stanley	2/15/2001	5 yr	Base	50
BPA	2/20/2001	Bal. '01	Op. Res.	
Enron	2/23/2001	3/30/2006	Peak	200
Merrill Lynch	3/1/2001	10 yr	Pk/Base	1000
PacifiCorp	3/1/2001	4 mos	Base	41
Duke	3/1/2001	4 mos	Base	100
Dynegy	3/1/2001	Bal '01	Peak	1000
Dynegy	3/1/2001	Bal. '01	OffPeak	*
PX BFM	3/1/2001	Bal. '01	Peak	525
Constellation	4/1/2001	2.25 yr	Peak	200
Powerex	4/1/2001	1.5 yr	Peak	400
Williams 1	4/1/2001	10 yr	Peak	300
Soledad	4/1/2001	3 yr	Base	13
PX BFM	4/1/2001	Bal. '01	Peak	925
Sempra	6/1/2001	10.3 yr	Peak	400
Primary Power	6/1/2001	2.5 yr	Base	16
Williams 2	6/1/2001	4.5 yr	Peak	400
Williams 3	6/1/2001	9.5 yr	Base	600
PacifiCorp	7/1/2001	10 yr	Base	400
Calpine 2	7/1/2001	9.5 yr	Base	1000
Alliance SRA	8/1/2001	10 yr	Sum. Peak	80
Calpine 3	8/1/2001	20 yr	Peak	495
Cal Peak	9/1/2001	10 yr	SSPeak	96
Cal Peak	9/1/2001	10 yr	SSPeak	144
Panda	9/1/2001	6 yr	Peak	142
Calpine 1	10/1/2001	10 yr	Base	1000
Cal Peak	11/1/2001	10 yr	Peak	96
Cal Peak	11/1/2001	10 yr	Peak	144
Dynegy	1/1/2002	3 yr	Base	200
Dynegy	1/1/2002	3 yr	Peak	600
Dynegy	1/1/2002	3 yr	Peak	1500
Dynegy	1/1/2002	3 yr	OffPeak	*
Duke	1/1/2002	9 yr	Base	300
Duke	1/1/2002	9 yr	Base	500
Avista	1/2/2002	9 yr	Base	100
Sempra	4/1/2002	9.5 yr	Base	1200
Constellation	7/1/2003	8.25 yr	Base	745
Total MW For All Agreements (Non-Coincident)				15,030
Maximum MW in Any Year				10,642
Total Agreements				40
Avg. Contract Price				$69

APPENDIX II

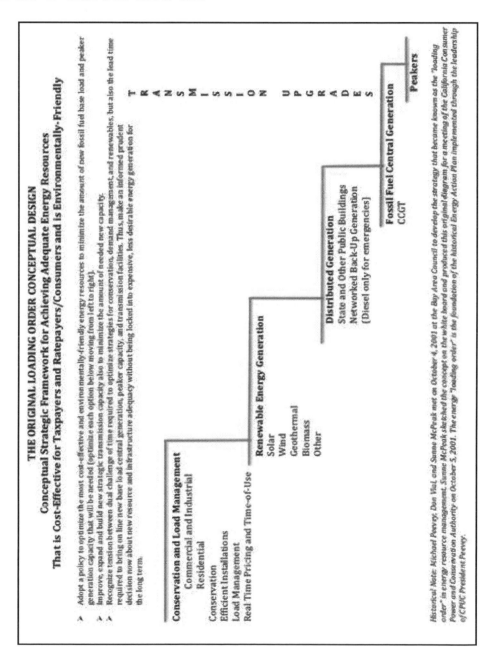

THE ORIGINAL LOADING ORDER CONCEPTUAL DESIGN

Conceptual Strategic Framework for Achieving Adequate Energy Resources
That Is Cost-Effective for Taxpayers and Ratepayers/Consumers and is Environmentally-Friendly

∧   Adopt a policy to optimize the most cost-effective and environmentally-friendly energy resources to minimize the amount of new fossil fuel base load and peaker generation capacity that will be needed (optimize each option below moving from left to right).

∧ ∧   Improve, expand and build new strategic transmission capacity also to minimize the amount of needed new capacity.

Recognize tension between dual challenge of time required to optimize strategies for conservation, demand management, and renewables, but also the lead time required to bring on line new base load central generation, peaker capacity, and transmission facilities. Thus, make an informed prudent decision now about new resource and infrastructure adequacy without being locked into expensive, less desirable energy generation for the long term.

Conservation and Load Management
   Commercial and Industrial
   Residential

Conservation
Efficient Installations
Load Management
Real Time Pricing and Time-of-Use

Renewable Energy Generation
Solar
Wind
Geothermal
Biomass
Other

Distributed Generation
State and Other Public Buildings
Networked Back-Up Generation
[Diesel only for emergencies]

Fossil Fuel Central Generation
CCGT

Peakers

TRANSMISSION → GRID ADDS

Historical Note: Michael Peevey, Dan Vial, and Sunne McPeak met on October 4, 2001 at the Bay Area Council to develop the strategy that became known as the "loading order" in energy resource management. Sunne McPeak sketched the concept on the white board and produced this original diagram for a meeting of the California Consumer Power and Conservation Authority on October 5, 2001. The energy "loading order" is the foundation of the historical Energy Action Plan implemented through the leadership of CPUC President Peevey.

APPENDIX III

Original Energy Action Plan, 2003
I. Optimize Energy Conservation and Resource Efficiency

California should decrease its per capital electricity use through increased energy conservation and efficiency measures. This would minimize the need for new generation, reduce emissions of toxic and criteria pollutants and greenhouse gases, avoid environmental concerns, improve energy reliability and contribute to price stability. Optimizing conservation and resource efficiency will include the following specific actions:

1. Implement a voluntary dynamic pricing system to reduce peak demand as much as 1,500 to 2,000 megawatts by 2007.
2. Improve new and remodeled building efficiency by 5 percent.
3. Improve air conditioner efficiency by 10% above federally mandated standards
4. Make every new state building a model of energy efficiency.
5. Create customer incentives for aggressive energy demand reduction.
6. Provide utilities with demand response and energy efficiency investment rewards comparable to the return on investment in new power and transmission projects.
7. Increase local government conservation and energy efficiency programs.
8. Incorporate, as appropriate per Public Resources Code section 25402, distributed generation or renewable technologies into energy efficiency standards for new building construction.
9. Encourage companies that invest in energy conservation and resource efficiency to register with the state's Climate Change Registry.

II. Accelerate the State's Goal for Renewable Generation
In 2002, the Governor signed the Renewable Portfolio Standard (RPS), SB 1078. This standard requires an annual increase in renewable generation equivalent to at least 1% of sales, with an aggregate goal of 20% by 2017. The state is aggressively implementing this policy, with the intention of accelerating the completion date to 2010, and will:

1. Add a net average of up to 600 MS of new renewable generation sources annually to the investor-owned utility resource portfolio.
2. Establish by June 30, 2003, key RPS implementation rules, including market price benchmarks, standard contract terms, flexible compliance and penalty mechanisms, and bid ranking criteria under the "least cost-best fit" rubric. Other key RPS rules will be developed and refined throughout 2003.
3. Facilitate an orderly and cost-effective expansion of the transmission system to connect potential renewable resources to load.
4. Initiate the development of RPS compliance rules for energy services providers and community choice aggregators.
5. Coordinate implementation with all relevant state agencies and with municipal utilities to facilitate their achievement of the standard.

III. Ensure Reliable, Affordable Electricity Generation
The state needs to ensure that its electrical generation system, including reserves, is sufficient to meet all current and future needs, and that this reliable and high quality electricity comes without over-reliance on a single fuel sources and at reasonable prices. To these ends the state will:

1. Add new generation resources to meet anticipated demand growth, modernize old, inefficient and dirty plants and achieve and maintain reserve levels in the 15 percent – 18 percent range. Current estimates show statewide need for 1500 – 2000 MW per year.

2. Finance a few critical power plants that the agencies conclude are necessary and would not otherwise be built. An estimated 300 MW of peaking capacity located in critical congestion and the need for new transmission lines.

3. Work with the California Independent System Operator (CAISO) to implement generator maintenance standards with an oversight process to support coordinated availability of generation.

4. Work with CAISO to ensure the development of a workable, competitive wholesale energy market that has meaningful market power mitigation rules.

5. Monitor the electricity market to identify any exercise of market power and manipulation, and work to improve FERC – established market rules to correct any observed abuses.

IV. Upgrade and Expand The Electricity Transmission and Distribution Infastructure

Reliable and reasonably priced electricity and natural gas, as well as increasing electricity from renewable resources, are dependent on a well-maintained and sufficient transmission and distribution system. The state will reinvigorate its planning, permitting, and funding processes to assure that necessary improvements and expansions to the distribution system and the built electricity grid are made on a timely basis:

1. The agencies will collaborate, in partnership with other state, local, and non-governmental agencies with energy responsibilities, in the California Energy Commission's integrated energy planning process to determine the statewide need for particular bulk transmission projects. This collaboration will build upon the California Independent System Operator's annual transmission plan and evaluate transmission, generation and demand side alternatives. It is intended to ensure that state objectives are evaluated and balanced in determining transmission investments that best meet the needs of California electricity users.

2. The Public Utilities Commission will issue an Order Instituting Rulemaking to propose changes to

3. its Certificate of Public Convenience and Necessity process, requiring under Public Utilities Code <>1001 et seq., in recognition of industry, marketplace, and legislative changes, like the creation of the CAISO and the directives of SB 1389. The Rulemaking will, among other things, propose to use the results of the Energy Commission's collaborative transmission assessment process to guide and fund IOU-sponsored transmission expansion or upgrade projects without having the PUC revisit questions of need for individual projects in certifying transmission improvements.

4. The Public Utilities Commission will ensure that IOUs build out and properly staff and maintain distribution systems to meet California's growth, provide reliable service, and stand ready to restore service after unplanned distribution system outages.

5. The Energy Commission will work with municipal utilities to help ensure completion of transmission expansion or upgrade projects in their systems for which the collaborative transmission assessment process finds a need.

V. Promote Customer and Utility Owned Distributed Generation

Distributed generation is an important local resource that can enhance reliability and provide high quality power, without compromising environmental quality. The state is promoting and encouraging clean and renewable customer and utility owned distributed generation as a key component of its energy system. Clean distributed generation should enhance the state's environmental goals. This determined and aggressive commitment to efficient, clean and renewable energy resources will provide vision and leadership to others seeking to enhance environmental quality and moderate energy sector impacts on climate change. Such resources, by their characteristics, are virtually guaranteed to serve California load. With proper inducements distributed generation will become economic.

1. Promote clean, small generation resources located at load centers.
2. Determine whether and how to hold distributed generation customers responsible for costs associated with Department of Water Resources power purchases.
3. Determine system benefits of distributed generation and related costs.
4. Develop standards so that renewable distributed generation may participate in the Renewable Portfolio Standard program.
5. Standardize definitions of eligible distributed generation technologies across agencies to better leverage programs and activities that encourage distributed generation.
6. Collaborate with the Air Resources Board, Cal-EPA and representatives of local air quality districts to achieve better integration of energy and air quality policies and regulations affecting distributed generation.
7. The agencies will work together to further develop distributed generation policies, target research and development, track the market adoption of distributed generation technologies, identify cumulative energy system impacts and examine issues associated with new technologies and their use.

VI. Ensure Reliable Supply of Reasonably Priced Natural Gas

The high and volatile price of natural gas contributed significantly to the energy crisis in 2000-2001 and concerns about manipulation of the market and scarcity persist. The Governor's Natural Gas Working Group was formed to monitor natural gas demand, supply and price issues and facilitate the construction of California infrastructure projects. Yet California remains vulnerable to the volatile spot market. The agencies will pursue the following actions:

1. Identify critical new gas transmission, distribution storage facilities needed to meet California's future needs.
2. Monitor the gas market to identify any exercise of market power and manipulation, and work to improve FERC-established market rules to correct any observed abuses.

3. Evaluate the net benefits of increasing the state's natural gas supply options, such as liquefied natural gas.
4. Support electric utilities and gas distribution companies entering into longer-term contracts as a hedge against volatile and high spot market prices.

In implementing this plan, the agencies are mindful that energy services – both natural gas and electric – are essential to every Californian's general welfare and to the health of California's economy. As actions to improve the reliability of these services are considered, the agencies will each take into account the effect the auction will have on energy expenditures, the environment and climate change, and the overall economy. Alternatives to proposed actions will be evaluated in an integrated fashion, consider the cost of action or inaction, and consider the equitable distribution of costs among customer classes and groups.

While implementation of this Action Plan represents a challenge, it is an important step for the agencies to take together to help achieve the state's overall goal of adequate, reliable, and reasonably priced electrical power and natural gas supplies.

Endnotes

1   Vekshin, A. (2016 Jun 14). "California Overtakes France to Become Sixth-Largest Economy." *Bloomberg.* Retrieved from: http://www.bloomberg.com/politics/articles/2016-06-14/california-overtakes-france-to-become-sixth-largest-economy

2   *Los Angeles Times.* (1962 September 30). Sec I, Pg 10.

3   Vara, V. (2015 Jan 8). How California Bested Texas. *New Yorker.* Retrieved from: http://www.newyorker.com/business/currency/california-bested-texas

4   Under 2 MOU. Retrieved from: http://under2mou.org/?page_id=10

5   R20 Regions of Climate Change. Projects. Retrieved from: http://regions20.org/projects/list

6   Megerian, C. & Finnegan, M. (2015 Apr 29). California's greenhouse gas emissions targets are getting tougher. *Los Angeles Times.* Retrieved from: http://www.latimes.com/local/political/la-me-pc-jerry-brown-orders-emission-targets-for-climate-change-20150429-story.html

7   U.S. Energy Information Administration. (2014 Dec 10). California leads the nation in the adoption of electric vehicles. Retrieved from: http://www.eia.gov/toda energy/detail.cfm?id=19131

8   California Energy Commission. (2015 April). *Appliance Energy Efficiency Standards.* Retrieved from: http://www.energy.ca.gov/commission/fact_sheets/documents/EE-Appliance_Energy_Efficiency_Standards.pdf

9   U.S. Energy Information Administration. (2015 Sep 17). *California.* Retrieved from: http://www.eia.gov/state/?sid=CA

10 Ibid.

11 Bureau of Labor Statistics. (2015 December). *Average Energy Prices.* Retrieved from: http://www.bls.gov/regions/west/news-release/averageenergyprices_losangeles.htm

12 NRDC. (2013 July). *California's Energy Efficiency Success Story.* Retrieved from: http://www.nrdc.org/energy/files/ca-success-story-FS.pdf

13 U.S. Energy Information Administration. (2014 Dec 10). California leads the nation in the adoption of electric vehicles.

Retrieved from: http://www.eia.gov/todayinenergy/detail.cfm?
id=19131

14   Shepardson, D. (2014 Dec 10). Report: Nearly half of EVs
     sold in California. *Detroit News*. Retrieved from: http://
     www.detroitnews.com/story/business/autos/2014/12/10/
     electric-vehicles/20193701/

15   McGreevy, P. (2015 Aug 23). California limits hybrid rebates to
     households earning less than $500,000. *Los Angeles Times*.
     Retrieved from: http://www.latimes.com/local/politics/la-me-
     pol-electric-cars-20150824-story.html

16   American Lung Association. Our Advocacy Victories. Retrieved
     from: http://www.lung.org/get-involved/become-an-advocate/
     our-victories.html

17   Florida, R. (2016 Jan 26). The Global Cities Where Tech Venture
     Capital Is Concentrated. *Atlantic*. Retrieved from: http://www.
     theatlantic.com/technology/archive/2016/01/global-startup-
     cities-venture-capital/429255/

18   Kirkham, C. (2015 Feb 2). California has one of the largest shares of
     high-tech workers in the U.S. *Los Angeles Times*. Retrieved from:
     http://www.latimes.com/business/la-fi-california-advanced-
     industries-20150202-story.html

19   Kirkham, C. (2016 Jan 2). California cranks out new businesses and
     jobs despite criticism. *Los Angeles Times*. Retrieved from: http://
     www.latimes.com/business/la-fi-business-climate-20160102-story.
     html

20   Next 10. (2014 May 22). Policy & clean tech innovation accel-
     erate consumer demand & spur additional economic growth.
     Retrieved from: http://next10.org/policy-clean-tech-innova-
     tion-accelerate-consumer-demand-spur-additional-econom-
     ic-growth

21   Kirkham, C. (2015 Jan 1). California's high housing costs drive
     out poor, middle-income workers. *Los Angeles Times*. Retrieved
     from: http://www.latimes.com/business/la-fi-california-migra-
     tion-20150101-story.html

22   Semuels, A. (2009 Jun 23). Losses of factory jobs in California
     blamed on regulation. *Los Angeles Times*. Retrieved from: http://
     www.latimes.com/business/la-fi-factory23-2009jun23-story.html

23   Varney, S. (2010 Oct 10). Companies Big Farewell to California. Fox Business. Retrieved from: http://www.foxbusiness.com/politics/2010/10/20/companies-bid-farewell-to-california.html

24   Hirsch, J. (2014 Mar 7). California positively gets a negative from Tesla on battery factory. *Los Angeles Times*. Retrieved from: http://articles.latimes.com/2014/mar/07/business/la-fi-tesla-battery-factory-20140307

25   U-T San Diego Editorial Board. (2013 May 26). Apple builds in Texas, not California. *San Diego Union-Tribune*. Retrieved from: http://www.sandiegouniontribune.com/news/2013/may/26/apple-builds-in-texas-not-california/

26   O'Reilly, R. (1983, Dec 16). Air board keeps smog rule on 1966-70 cars. *Los Angeles Times (1923-Current File)*.

27   Fisher, D. (1973, Jun 10). The catalytic converter---a costly 'pill'. *Los Angeles Times (1923-Current File)*.

28   Fisher, D. (1975, Mar 08). Air board votes to keep catalytic units for autos. *Los Angeles Times (1923-Current File)*.

29   California Environmental Protection Agency, Air Resources Board. (2014). *Zero-Emission Vehicle Legal and Regulatory Activities and Background*. Retrieved from: http://www.arb.ca.gov/msprog/zevprog/zevregs/zevregs.htm

30   Hirsch, J. (2015, Aug 5). Tesla's push for tougher emission standards would boost it bottom line. *Los Angeles Times*. Retrieved from: http://www.latimes.com/business/autos/la-fi-tesla-credits-20150805-story.html

31   Weinberg, D. (2015, May 8). Tesla's secret to success? Selling emission credits. *Marketplace*. Retrieved from: http://www.marketplace.org/2013/05/08/sustainability/teslas-secret-success-selling-emissions-credits

32   Department of Finance. 2016-2017 Governor's Budget, Air Resources Board. Retrieved from: http://www.ebudget.ca.gov/2016-17/StateAgencyBudgets/3890/3900/department.html

33   Department of Finance. 2016-2017 Governor's Budget, Public Utilities Commission. Retrieved from: http://www.ebudget.ca.gov/2016-17/StateAgencyBudgets/8000/8660/department.html

34   Department of Finance. 2016-2017 Governor's Budget, Energy Resource Conservation and Development Commission. Retrieved from: http://www.ebudget.ca.gov/2016-17/State AgencyBudgets/3000/3360/department.html

35   California Department of Finance. (2016). Retrieved from: http://www.bloomberg.com/politics/articles/2016-06-14/california-overtakes-france-to-become-sixth-largest-economy

36   Vekshin, A. (2016, June 14). California Overtakes France to Become Sixth Largest Economy. Bloomberg. Retrieved from: http://www.bloomberg.com/politics/articles/2016-06-14/california-overtakes-france-to-become-sixth-largest-economy

37   Hackett, R. (2015, Jun 15). States with the most Fortune 500 companies. *Fortune Magazine.* Retrieved from: http://fortune.com/2015/06/15/states-most-fortune-500-companies/

38   *Governing Magazine.* Retrieved from: http://www.governing.com/gov-data/military-civilian-active-duty-employee-work-force-numbers-by-state.html

39   Public Policy Institute of California. (2012). *California's Political Geography.* Retrieved from: http://www.ppic.org/main/publica-tion_quick.asp?i=1007

40   Stanfield, J. (2010). California votes down proposition 23 in show of support for greenhouse gas limits. *SNL Generation Markets Week.*

41   United States Census Bureau 2010

42   Southern California Public Radio. (2013). 10 Fun Facts about California's Noble Prize winners. Retrieved from: http://www.scpr.org/news/2013/10/10/39736/10-fun-facts-about-california-s-nobel-prize-winner/

43   Walker, T. (2013 July 12). The billionaire factory: Why Stanford University produces so many celebrated web entrepreneurs. *Independent.* Retrieved from: http://www.independent.co.uk/student/news/the-billionaire-factory-why-stanford-university-produces-so-many-celebrated-web-entrepreneurs-8706573.html

44   Ramirez, L. (2015 Aug 25). San Jose State Alums Beat Out Elite School Grads for Tech Jobs. *CBS.* Retrieved from: http://san-francisco.cbslocal.com/2015/08/25/san-jose-state-university-sjsu-silicon-valley-tech-jobs-apple-cisco-hewlett-packard/

45   Pickoff-White, L. & Bowe, R. (2015 Jun 23). Independent Study Condemns System of Communication Between Utilities and Their Regulators. *KQED News*. Retrieved from: http://ww2.kqed.org/news/2015/06/23/independent-study-condemns-system-of-communications-between-utilities-and-their-regulators

46   Weare, Christopher. (2003). The California Electricity Crisis: Causes and Policy Options. *Public Policy Institute of California*. Retrieved from: http://www.ppic.org/content/pubs/report/R_103CWR.pdf

47   Young, S. Competition in the Generation, Sale and Transmission of Electric Energy. Nevada Legislature. Retrieved from: https://leg.state.nv.us/Division/Research/Publications/Bkground/BP95-16.pdf

48   California Public Utilities Commission. Telecommunications & Broadband. Retrieved from: http://www.cpuc.ca.gov/communications/

49   Rodriguez, J. (2016 Jan 25). Sweeping new regulations proposed for Uber, Lyft may level playing field for taxis. *San Francisco Examiner*. Retrieved from: http://www.sfexaminer.com/more-inspections-criminal-checks-in-sweeping-new-ca-regulations-for-uber-lyft/

50   Mazza, S. (2015 Mar 3). Election 2015: Hermosa Beach Voters soundly reject Measure O's oil-drilling proposal. *Daily Breeze*. Retrieved from: http://www.dailybreeze.com/government-and-politics/20150303/election-2015-hermosa-beach-voters-soundly-reject-measure-os-oil-drilling-proposal

51   Fonseca, D. (2011 Apr 25). Crucial 710 Freeway Vote Goes Before Assembly Today. *Eagle Rock Patch*. Retrieved from: http://patch.com/california/eaglerock/crucial-710-freeway-vote-goes-before-assembly-today

52   Pitts, J. & Stephens, E. (1978). Arie Jan Haagen-Smit. *Air Pollution Control Association*. Retrieved from: http://www.arb.ca.gov/research/hsawards/japcaarticle1978.pdf

53   South Coast AQMD. The Southland's War on Smog: Fifty Years of Progress Toward Clean Air. Retrieved from: http://www.aqmd.gov/home/library/public-information/publications/50-years-of-progress

54   Cannon, L. *Governor Reagan His Rise to Power*, PublicAffairs, 2003, Pg. 177.

55   Rosenberg, J. (2012 Jun 25). Why California's Beaches are Open to Everyone. *KCET Los Angeles.* Retrieved from: http://www.kcet.org/socal/departures/columns/laws-that-shaped-la/why-californias-beaches-are-open-to-everyone.html

56   Nixon, R. (1973 Nov 7). 323 – Address to the Nation About Policies to Deal with the Energy Shortage. Retrieved from: http://www.presidency.ucsb.edu/ws/?pid=4034

57   Brown, S. (1998 Mar 30). The Automakers Big-Time Bet on Fuel Cells. *Fortune Magazine.* Retrieved from: http://archive.fortune.com/magazines/fortune/fortune_archive/1998/03/30/240114/index.htm

58   U.S. Energy Information Administration. (2015 Mar 24). California first state to generate more than 5% of electricity from utility-scale solar. Retrieved from: http://www.eia.gov/todayinenergy/detail.cfm?id=20492

59   Nolte, C. (1999 May 16). Boomers, Beats and Baseball/ The generation that came home from World War II rolled up their sleeves, changed the country and reinvented California. *SF Gate.* Retrieved from: http://www.sfgate.com/news/article/Boomers-Beats-and-Baseball-The-generation-that-2930456.php

60   Tellier, Luc-Normand. *Urban world history: An economic and geographical perspective.* PUQ, 2009.

61   Rasmussen, C. (2003, Mar. 23). "Did Auto, Oil Conspiracy Put the Brakes on Trolleys?" *Los Angeles Times.* Retrieved from: http://www.latimes.com/me-2003-los-angeles-streetcar-history-story.html

62   Gardner, S. (2014 Jul 14). LA Smog: the battle against air pollution. *Marketplace.* Retrieved from: http://www.marketplace.org/2014/07/14/sustainability/we-used-be-china/la-smog-battle-against-air-pollution

63   Obama, B. (2016 Jan 14). "Remarks by the President in State of the Union Rollout Town Hall." The White House Office of the Press Secretary. Retrieved from: https://www.whitehouse.gov/the-press-office/2016/01/14/remarks-president-state-union-rollout-town-hall

64 McNally, J. (2010 Jul 26). July 26, 1943: L.A. gets first big smog. *Wired Magazine*. Retrieved from: http://www.wired.com/2010/07/0726la-first-big-smog/

65 Gardner, S. (2014 Jul 14). LA Smog: the battle against air pollution.

66 Roosevelt, M. (2011 May 2). California's right to exceed federal auto emissions standards is upheld. *Los Angeles Times*. Retrieved from: http://articles.latimes.com/2011/may/02/local/la-me-clean-cars-20110502

67 Barboza, T. (2014 Oct 22). Hot, stagnant weather in 2014 blamed for more bad air days in the Southland. *Los Angeles Times*. Retrieved from: http://www.latimes.com/local/lanow/la-me-ln-bad-air-days-smog-los-angeles-20141022-story.html

68 Sherman, Joe. *Charging Ahead*. Oxford University Press, USA, 1998.

69 Mai-Duc, C. (2015 May 20). The 1969 Santa Barbara oil spill that changed oil and gas exploration forever. *Los Angeles Times*. Retrieved from: http://www.latimes.com/local/lanow/la-me-ln-santa-barbara-oil-spill-1969-20150520-htmlstory.html

70 Clarke, K. C. and Jeffrey J. Hemphill. (2002). The Santa Barbabra Oil Spill, A Retrospective. Yearbook of the Association of Pacific Coast Geographers, Editor Darrick Danta, University of Hawai'i Press, vol. 64, pp. 157-162. Retrieved from: http://www.geog.ucsb.edu/~kclarke/Papers/SBOilSpill1969.pdf

71 Clarke, K. C. and Jeffrey J. Hemphill. (2002). The Santa Barbabra Oil Spill, A Retrospective. Yearbook of the Association of Pacific Coast Geographers, Editor Darrick Danta, University of Hawai'i Press, vol. 64, pp. 157-162. Retrieved from: http://www.geog.ucsb.edu/~kclarke/Papers/SBOilSpill1969.pdf

72 McDougal, Dennis. *Privileged Son: Otis Chandler And The Rise And Fall Of The L.A. Times Dynasty*, Da Capo Press, USA, 2009.

73 Corwin, M. (1989 Jan 28). The Oil Spill Heard 'Round the Country! *Los Angeles Times*. Retrieved from: http://www2.bren.ucsb.edu/~dhardy/1969_Santa_Barbara_Oil_Spill/Home.html

74 Callahan, M. (2014 Aug 22). Sea Ranch beach reopened to public after 11 years. *Press Democrat*. Retrieved from: http://www.pressdemocrat.com/news/2553533-181/sea-ranch-beach-reopened-to?artslide=0

75 Sonoma Magazine Staff. (2015 Feb 3). Nuclear Fault Line – Bodega Head. *Sonoma Magazine.* Retrieved from: http://www.sonomamag.com/nuclear-fault-line/

76 Little, Charles E. *Greenways for America.* JHU Press, 1995. Pg 72

77 California State Lands Commission. *Oil and Gas Leases.* Retrieved from: http://www.slc.ca.gov/Info/Oil_Gas.html

78 California Natural Resources Agency. Frequently Asked Question about CEQA. Retrieved from: http://resources.ca.gov/ceqa/more/faq.html

79 Nagourney, A. (2015 May 16). Brown's Arid California, Thanks Partly to His Father. *New York Times.* Retrieved from: http://www.nytimes.com/2015/05/17/us/jerry-browns-arid-california-thanks-partly-to-his-father.html

80 Johns, Andrew L., ed. *A Companion to Ronald Reagan.* Vol. 61. John Wiley & Sons, 2014.

81 Cannon, L. (1991). *President Reagan: The role of a lifetime.* PublicAffairs.

82 Cannon, L. *Governor Reagan: His Rise to Power.* PublicAffairs, 2005, Pg 303.

83 Calavita, N. (1995). California Environmental Goals and Policy Part 1. Center for California Studies, California State University.

84 Fosler, R. S. (1991). *The new economic role of American states: Strategies in a competitive world economy.* Oxford University Press. Pg 214.

85 California Energy Commission. (2011). Renewable Power in California: Status and Issues. Retrieved from: http://www.energy.ca.gov/2011publications/CEC-150-2011-002/CEC-150-2011-002-LCF-REV1.pdf

86 McGrory, M. (1978). Anti-Nuclear Forces Win in California. Toledo Blade. Retrieved from: https://news.google.com/newspapers?nid=1350&dat=19780314&id=qg5PAAAAIBAJ&sjid=aQIEAAAAIBAJ&pg=5622,6088423&hl=en

87 Penn, I. and Masunaga, S. (2016 June 21). "PG&E to Close Diablo Canyon, California's Last Nuclear Power Plant." *Los Angeles Times.* Retrieved from: http://www.latimes.com/business/la-fi-diablo-canyon-nuclear-20160621-snap-story.html

88   Groves, M. (1991). Bay Area Lawyer is Energetic in Efforts to Conserve Energy. *Los Angeles Times*. Retrieved from: http://articles.latimes.com/1991-04-22/business/fi-464_1_energy-efficiency

89   Wellock, Thomas Raymond. *Critical Masses: Opposition to Nuclear Power in California, 1958-1978*. Univ of Wisconsin Press, 1998.

90   Kemp, R. P. M., Arie Rip, and J. W. Schot. "Constructing transition paths through the management of niches." (2001): 269-299. Retrieved from: http://doc.utwente.nl/42568/1/Kemp01constructing.PDF

91   The National Museum of American History. The Public Utility Regulatory Policies Act. Retrieved from: http://americanhistory.si.edu/powering/past/history4.htm

92   Solar Energy Industries Association. (2015 Jun 15). California Surges Ahead in Solar Capacity; Cracks 10,000 MW Mark. Retrieved from: https://www.seia.org/news/california-surges-ahead-solar-capacity-cracks-10000-mw-mark

93   Hays, J. (1986 Jan). In Memoriam: Leonard Ross. Ecology Law Quarterly. Retrieved from: http://scholarship.law.berkeley.edu/cgi/viewcontent.cgi?article=1276&context=elq

94   Pechman, Carl. *Regulating Power: The Economics of Electrictiy in the Information Age: The Economics of Electricity in the Information Age*. Vol. 15. Springer Science & Business Media, 2012.

95   Eto, Joseph, Steven Stoft, and Timothy Belden. "The theory and practice of decoupling utility revenues from sales." *Utilities Policy* 6.1 (1997): 43-55.

96   Migden-Ostrander, J., Watson, B., Lamont, D., and Sedano, R. (2014) Decoupling Case Studies: Revenue Regulation Implementation in Six States. Montpelier, VT: The Regulatory Assistance Project. Retrieved from: http://www.raponline.org/document/download/id/7209

97   The Hour. (1982 Apr 16). Solar One Makes Shining Debut. Retrieved from: https://news.google.com/newspapers?nid=1916&dat=19820416&id=YhFJAAAAIBAJ&sjid=oQUNAAAAIBAJ&pg=3866,2864017&hl=en

98   Electric Power Research Institute. (1990 Dec 11). Cool Water Coal Gasification Program: Final Report.

99   Wittenberg, D. Eyewitness account.

100   Immel, A. Richard. (1976). The Big Stick: California's Air Board Breaks New Ground with Pollution Limits. *Wall Street Journal.* June 9, Pg. 1.

101   Isser, S. (2015). *Electricity Restructuring in the United States: Markets and Policy from the 1978 Energy Act to the Present.* Cambridge University Press.

102   Clifton, J., Lanthier, P., & Schröter, H. (Eds.). (2014). *The Economic and Social Regulation of Public Utilities: An International History.* Routledge.

103   Lambert, J. D. (2015). *The Power Brokers: The Struggle to Shape and Control the Electric Power Industry.* MIT Press.

104   Isser, S. (2015). *Electricity Restructuring in the United States: Markets and Policy from the 1978 Energy Act to the Present.* Cambridge University Press.

105   Morian, D. (1996 Aug 31). Assembly Oks Bill to Deregulate Electricity. *Los Angeles Times.* Retrieved from: http://articles.latimes.com/1996-08-31/news/mn-39301_1_electrical-deregulation

106   Sweeney, J. L. (2002). *The California electricity crisis.* Hoover Press.

107   Ibid.

108   Clifton, J., Lanthier, P., & Schröter, H. (Eds.). (2014). *The Economic and Social Regulation of Public Utilities: An International History.* Routledge.

109   Hua, V. (1997 Nov 25). Edison Sells 10 Gas-Fired Plants. *Los Angeles Times.* Retrieved from: http://articles.latimes.com/1997/nov/25/business/fi-57429

110   Kraul, C. (1997 Nov 14). Ralphs Defects From Edison, Signs With New Power Source. *Los Angeles Times.* Retrieved from: http://articles.latimes.com/1997/nov/14/business/fi-53558

111   Brooks, N. (1998 May 15). New Energy Ventures Wins Military Contract. *Los Angeles Times.* Retrieved from: http://articles.latimes.com/1998/may/15/business/fi-49866

112 Raine, G. (1998 Mar 29). Deflating Deregulation. *SF Gate*. Retrieved from: http://www.sfgate.com/business/article/ DEFLATING-DEREGULATION-3098055.php

113 Ibid.

114 Brennan, T. (2001 Oct). Questioning The Conventional "Wisdom". Cato Institute. Retrieved from: http://object.cato. org/sites/cato.org/files/serials/files/regulation/2001/10/special- report2.pdf

115 Faruqui, A and Eakin, K. (2002). Electricity Pricing in Transition. Kluwer Academic Publishers.

116 McSwain, D. (2004 Jan 23). SDG&E settles charges of mar- ket manipulation. *San Diego Union-Tribune*. Retrieved from: http://www.sandiegouniontribune.com/news/2004/jan/23/ sdge-settles-charges-of-market-manipulation/

117 Said, C. (2003 Apr 27). Buckets of trouble/Tracking down the billions of dollars of the energy crisis cost California. *SF Gate*. Retrieved from: http://www.sfgate.com/business/article/ Buckets-of-trouble-Tracking-down-the-billions-2620034.php

118 Lockyer, B. (2004 Apr). Attorney General's Energy White Paper, A Law Enforcement Perspective on the California Energy Crisis. Office of the Attorney General. Retrieved from: http://www. ag.ca.gov/publications/energywhitepaper.pdf

119 Ibid.

120 McNamara, W. (2002). *California Energy Crisis: Lessons for a Deregulating Industry*. PennWell Books.

121 Oppel, Jr, R. (2002 May 8). Enron's Many Strands: The Strategies; How Enron got California to Buy Power It Didn't Need. *New York Times*. Retrieved from: http://www.nytimes.com/2002/05/08/ business/enron-s-many-strands-strategies-enron-got-california- buy-power-it-didn-t-need.html

122 Morian, D. (2000 Dec 31). Davis Faces Growing Criticism on Power Crisis. *Los Angeles Times*. Retrieved from: http://articles. latimes.com/2000/dec/31/news/mn-6834

123 Sanchez, R. & Booth, W. (2001 Jan 14). California's Energy Future Looks Dim. *Washington Post*. Retrieved from: https://www. washingtonpost.com/archive/politics/2001/01/14/californias- energy-future-looks-dim/bf8ff551-d11f-4ff1-8f58-a210d1dcae4b/

124 Ibid.

125 Ibid.

126 Eichenwald, K. (2005). *Conspiracy of fools: A true story.* Broadway.

127 Zacchino, N. (2016) Interview with Gray Davis. Retrieved from: *California Comeback: How a "Failed State" Became a Model for the Nation.* Thomas Dunne Books, St. Martin's Press, page 100.

128 Ibid.

129 Lockyer, B. (2004 Apr). Attorney General's Energy White Paper. Office of the Attorney General.

130 Douglass, E. (2006 Mar 17). Utilities Sue DWP over Power Deals. *Los Angeles Times.* Retrieved from: http://articles.latimes.com/2006/mar/17/business/fi-powersuit17

131 McNamara, W. (2002). *California Energy Crisis: Lessons for a Deregulating Industry.* PennWell Books.

132 Farnsworth, E. (Interviewer) & Davis, G. (Interviewee). (2001 Jan 25). Power Crisis in California [Interview Transcript]. PBS Newshour. Retrieved from: http://www.pbs.org/newshour/bb/business-jan-june01-davis_1-25/

133 Ibid.

134 Fellmeth, R. (2001 Nov). Plunging Into Darkness: Energy Deregulation Collides with Scarcity. Center for Public Interest Law, University of San Diego, School of Law. Retrieved from: http://www.cpil.org/download/PUC.BF.speech.Nov2001.pdf

135 Bustillo, M. (2001 Jan 25). Wall Street Firm's Web Site Calls Blackouts a Tactic to Raise Rates. Los Angeles Times. Retrieved from: http://articles.latimes.com/2001/jan/25/news/mn-17441

136 Peevey, Michael. Eyewitness account.

137 Warren, J. & Morian, D. (2001 Sept 23). Political Odd Couple in Tiff Over Edison. *Los Angeles Times.* Retrieved from: http://articles.latimes.com/2001/sep/23/local/me-48906

138 Rau, J. (2005 Aug 22). Gov. Enacts Few Reform Proposals. Los Angeles Times. Retrieved from: http://articles.latimes.com/2005/aug/22/local/me-cpr22

139 Ingram, C. & Morian, D. (2001 Feb 21). Senate Oks Forming State Power Agency. *Los Angeles Times.* Retrieved from: http://articles.latimes.com/2001/feb/21/news/mn-28242

140 Vogel, N. (2001 Dec 27). Power Contracts Improved After Freeman Left. *Los Angeles Times*. Retrieved from: http://articles.latimes.com/2001/dec/27/local/me-18344

141 Ibid.

142 Federal Energy Regulatory Commission. (2002 Jan). Report on the Economic Impacts on Western Utilities and Ratepayers of Price Caps on Spot Market Sales. Retrieved from: https://www.ferc.gov/legal/maj-ord-reg/land-docs/Congressional-report.pdf

143 Alonso-Zaldivar, R. (2001 Aug 15). Bush Selects Ex-Texas Regulator to Head FERC. *Los Angeles Times*. Retrieved from: http://articles.latimes.com/2001/aug/15/news/mn-34361

144 Behr, P. (2001 Apr 27). FERC Taken to Task Over Calif. Energy Crisis. *Washington Post*. Retrieved from: https://www.washingtonpost.com/archive/business/2001/04/27/ferc-taken-to-task-over-calif-energy-crisis/82ea53d3-9beb-4373-936d-5ad64bf-6ccc9/

145 Goswami, D. Y., & Kreith, F. (Eds.). (2007). *Handbook of energy efficiency and renewable energy*. Crc Press.

146 Ibid.

147 Ibid.

148 Bachrach, D., Ardema, M., & Leupp, A. (2003). Energy efficiency leadership in California. Natural Resources Defense Council. Retrieved from: https://www.nrdc.org/air/energy/eecal/eecal.pdf

149 Ritschel, A., & Smestad, G. P. (2003). Energy subsidies in California's electricity market deregulation. *Energy Policy*, *31*(13), 1379-1391.

150 U.S. Energy Information Administration. (May 2010). California Restructuring Suspended

151 http://docs.cpuc.ca.gov/published/REPORT/6571.htm

152 U.S. Energy Information Administration. (May 2010). California Restructuring Suspended

153 Reiterman, T., & Brooks, N. (2001). $5.7- Billion Energy Rate Hike is Okd. *Los Angeles Times*. Retrieved from: https://www.caiso.com/Documents/AttachmentH08-Jun-01.pdf

154 Office of Ratepayer Advocates. California Residential Electric Rate Redesign. State of California. Retrieved from: http://www.dra.ca.gov/general.aspx?id=2444

155 U.S. Energy Information Administration. Subsequent Events California's Energy Crisis. Retrieved from: http://www.eia.gov/electricity/policies/legislation/california/subsequentevents.html

156 Holson, L. (2001 Apr 6). California's Largest Utility Files for Bankruptcy. *New York Times*. Retrieved from: http://www.nytimes.com/2001/04/07/us/california-s-largest-utility-files-for-bankruptcy.html

157 Reiterman, T. (2001 Dec 01). PG&E Seeks Ok for Reorganization. *Los Angeles Times*. Retrieved from: http://articles.latimes.com/2001/dec/01/local/me-10283

158 Ibid.

159 Holson, L. (2001 April 7). California's Largest Utility Files for Bankruptcy. *New York Times*.

160 Ibid.

161 Brooks, N. & Reiterman, T. (2003 Dec 19). Regulators OK Plan for PG&E Recovery. *Los Angeles Times*. Retrieved from: http://articles.latimes.com/2003/dec/19/business/fi-pge19

162 California Planning & Development Report. (2004 May) Public Gains 140,000 Acres of PG&E Land. Retrieved from: http://www.cp-dr.com/node/613

163 Pacific Gas & Electric Company. (2003 Dec 19). Order Instituting Investigation into the ratemaking implications for Pacific Gas and Electric Company (PG&E) pursuant to the Commission's Alternative Plan of Reorganization under Chapter 11 of the Bankruptcy Code for PG&E, in the United States Bankruptcy Court, Northern District of California, San Francisco Division, In re Pacific Gas and Electric Company, Case No. 01-30923 DM. Retrieved from: https://www.pge.com/includes/docs/pdfs/shared/environment/pge/stewardship/cpuc_settlementagrement.pdf

164 Ibid.

165 Brooks, N. & Reiterman, T. (2003 Dec 19). Regulators OK Plan for PG&E Recovery. *Los Angeles Times*.

166 Southern California Edison. (2001 April 6). SCE Responds to PG&E Bankruptcy Filing. Retrieved from: http://newsroom.edison.com/releases/sce-responds-to-pg-e-bankruptcy-filing

167 Hirsch, J. (2001 Sept 02). Idea of Edison Bankruptcy Gains Currency. *Los Angeles Times*. Retrieved from: http://articles.latimes.com/2001/sep/02/business/fi-41123

168 Sweeney, J. L. (2002). *The California electricity crisis*. Hoover Press.

169 California Public Utilities Commission. (2001 Oct 2). PUC and Edison settle federal litigation to maintain utility service without raising rates. Retrieved from: http://docs.cpuc.ca.gov/published/NEWS_RELEASE/10081.htm

170 Southern California Edison. (2001 Oct 2). SCE Comments on Settlement with PUC re: Filed Rate Doctrine Lawsuit to Restore Utility's Financial Health. Retrieved from: http://newsroom.edison.com/releases/sce-comments-on-settlement-with-cpuc-re:-filed-rate-doctrine-lawsuit-to-restore-utility-8217;s-financial-health

171 Securities and Exchange Commission. (2003 Aug 25). Current Report: Pursuant to Section 13 or 15(d) of the Securities Exchange Act of 1934. Retrieved from: http://www.sec.gov/Archives/edgar/data/75488/000100498003000204/final0825.htm

172 *Silicon Valley Business Journal*. (2002 Feb 27). PUC Commissioner Bilas Resigns. Retrieved from: http://www.bizjournals.com/san-jose/stories/2002/02/25/daily53.html

173 Coleman, J. (2003, Jan 01). Ex-Edison exec picked for PUC. *Daily Breeze*

174 Governor's Conservation Team. The Summer 2001 Conservation Report. California State and Consumer Services Agency, California Energy Commission. Retrieved from: http://www.energy.ca.gov/reports/CEC-400-2002-001/CEC-400-2002-001.PDF

175 Ibid.

176 Sweeney, J. L. (2002). *The California electricity crisis*. Hoover Press.

177 California Energy Commission. (2005 July). Implementing California's Loading Order for Electricity Resources. Retrieved from: http://www.energy.ca.gov/2005publications/CEC-400-2005-043/CEC-400-2005-043.PDF

178 Wallack, T. (2002 May 4). Reprieve for utility regulator/Duque may stay longer at PUC. *SF Gate*. Retrieved from: http://www.sf-gate.com/business/article/Reprieve-for-utility-regulator-Duque-may-stay-2842360.php

179 Lifsher, M. (2004 Nov 23). Suit Names the PUC's Lynch. *Los Angeles Times*. Retrieved from: http://articles.latimes.com/2004/nov/23/business/fi-lynch23

180 Reiterman, T. (2003 Jan 01). Davis Replaces PUC Chief. *Los Angeles Times*. Retrieved from: http://articles.latimes.com/2003/jan/01/local/me-puc1

181 California Energy Commission. (2003). State of California Energy Action Plan. State of California. Retrieved from: http://www.energy.ca.gov/energy_action_plan/2003-05-08_ACTION_PLAN.PDF

182 Ibid.

183 California Energy Commission. State of California Energy Action Plan. Retrieved from: http://www.energy.ca.gov/energy_action_plan/

184 Ibid.

185 Ibid.

186 Matek, B. & Gawell, K. (2014 Feb). Report on the State of Geothermal Energy in California. Geothermal Energy Association. Retrieved from: http://geo-energy.org/events/California percent20Status percent20Report percent20February percent202014 percent20Final.pdf

187 California Energy Commission. Overview of Wind Energy in California. State of California. Retrieved from: http://www.energy.ca.gov/wind/overview.html

188 California Energy Commission. Renewable Energy. Retrieved from: http://www.energy.ca.gov/renewables/*tracking*_progress/documents/renewable.pdf

189 Vogel, N. (2002 Sept 13). Davis signs Bill Boosting Clean Energy. *Los Angeles Times*. Retrieved from: http://articles.latimes.com/2002/sep/13/local/me-bills13

190 Ibid.

191 California Energy Commission. (2006). Senate Bill No. 107. State of California. Retrieved from: http://www.energy.ca.gov/portfolio/documents/documents/sb_107_bill_20060926_chaptered.pdf

192 Repperger, D. W. (2008). Electricity from Renewable Resources--Status, Prospects, and Impediments. *The Ohio Journal of Science, 108*(5), 113-114.

193 Hilton, S. & Martin, J. (2011 Apr 13). Renewable Energy Law Alert: Governor Brown Signs Bill Increasing California's Renewable Portfolio Standard to 33%. Stoel Rives LLP. Retrieved from: http://www.stoel.com/renewable-energy-law-alert-governor-brown-signs-bill

194 Ibid.

195 Yamamura, K. (2005 Apr 30). California seeks to boost image of home solar power. Sacramento Bee. Retrieved from: http://articles.chicagotribune.com/2005-04-30/news/0504300230_1_solar-panels-solar-power-solar-program

196 Taylor, J. (2005 Dec 1). Million Solar Roofs Bill Dies in California Assembly. Heartland. Retrieved from: https://www.heartland.org/news-opinion/news/million-solar-roofs-bill-dies-in-california-assembly

197 Ibid.

198 Hoschchild, D. (2005 Sept 9). Where does California's Million Solar Roofs Initiative Go From Here? The Vote Solar Initiative. Retrieved from: http://www.renewableenergyworld.com/articles/2005/09/where-does-californias-million-solar-roofs-initiative-go-from-here-36390.html

199 Carver, B., & Kian, S. (2008). California Solar Initiative: How Mandatory Time-of-Use Rates Chilled the Solar Energy Market, The. *Stan. L. & Pol'y Rev.*, *19*, 384.

200 California Public Utilities Commission. About the California Solar Initiative. Retrieved from: http://www.cpuc.ca.gov/General.aspx?id=6133

201 Ibid.

202 Go Solar California. (2005 Dec 5). December 15, 2005: PUC Increases Funding for Solar Technologies. News Releases and Announcements. Retrieved from: http://www.gosolarcalifornia.ca.gov/news_media/newsreleases.php

203 Go Solar California. (2005 Dec 5). PUC Creates Groundbreaking Solar Energy Program. News Releases and Announcements. Retrieved from: http://docs.cpuc.ca.gov/published/NEWS_RELEASE/52745.htm

204 Ibid.

205 Carver, B., & Kian, S. (2008). California Solar Initiative: How Mandatory Time-of-Use Rates Chilled the Solar Energy Market, The. *Stan. L. & Pol'y Rev.*, *19*, 384.

206 Go Solar California! (2007 Sept 12). Update on the PUC California Solar Initiative Program Administration. Retrieved from: http://www.gosolarcalifornia.ca.gov/news_media/program_updates/2007-09-12_PROGRAM_UPDATE.PDF

207 California Public Utilities Commission. About the California Solar Initiative. State of California. Retrieved from: http://www.cpuc.ca.gov/General.aspx?id=6047

208 Ibid.

209 Ibid.

210 Rickerson, W., Bennhold, F., & Bradbury, J. (2008). Feed-in tariffs and renewable energy in the USA: A policy update. *Raleigh, NC, Washington, DC, and Hamburg, Germany: North Carolina Solar Center, Heinrich Böll Foundation North America, and the World Future Council.*

211 Bull, P. (2014 Jun 20). California's Landmark Solar Deployment Program – the CA Solar Initiative – has Successfully Lifted the State's Distributed Solar Industry into Orbit. NRDC. Retrieved from: https://www.nrdc.org/experts/pierre-bull/californias-landmark-solar-deployment-program-ca-solar-initiative-has

212 California Public Utilities Commission. (2006 May 25). Order Affirming ALJ's Ruling Reducing Solar PV Incentives. Retrieved from: http://docs.cpuc.ca.gov/PUBLISHED/FINAL_DECISION/56805.htm

213 CPUC. (2006 Jan 12). Revised Joint Staff Proposal to Implement A California Solar Initiative. Retrieved from: http://docs.cpuc.ca.gov/PublishedDocs/WORD_PDF/FINAL_DECISION/52902.PDF

214 Lacey, S. (2014 Nov 4). The End of a Solar Era: The Legacy of the California Solar Initiative. Greentech Media. Retrieved from: http://www.greentechmedia.com/articles/read/the-legacy-of-the-california-solar-initiative

215 California Solar Statistics. Data Downloads. Retrieved from: https://www.californiasolarstatistics.ca.gov/data_downloads/

216 California Public Utilities Commission. The CSI Research, Development and Deployment (RD&D) Plan. Retrieved from: http://www.cpuc.ca.gov/General.aspx?id=6071

217 PR Newswire. (2007 Apr 8). Newsweek Cover: Save the Planet – or Else. Retrieved from: http://www.prnewswire.com/

news-releases/newsweek-cover-save-the-planet----or-else-57933962.html

218 California Air Resources Board. Assembly Bill 32 Overview. Retrieved from: http://www.arb.ca.gov/cc/ab32/ab32.htm

219 Ibid.

220 Ibid.

221 Athens, L. (2012). *Building an Emerald City: A guide to creating green building policies and programs.* Island Press.

222 Woody, T. (2014 May 2). Arnold Schwarzenegger's Dream Fuel Makes a Comeback. *Atlantic.* Retrieved from: http://www.theatlantic.com/technology/archive/2014/05/california-just-launched-a-hydrogen-car-revolution/361592/

223 Schwarzenegger, A. Protecting the Environment and Promoting Clean Energy. Retrieved from: http://www.schwarzenegger.com/issues/milestone/protecting-the-environment-and-promoting-clean-energy

224 Grunwald, M. (2008 Sept 24). Arnold Schwarzenegger. *Time Magazine.* Retrieved from: http://content.time.com/time/specials/packages/article/0,28804,1841778_1841779_1841796,00.html

225 Prodhan, G. (2013 Feb 1). Arnold Schwarzenegger Credits Green Activism to Simple Upbringing in Austria. Reuters. Retrieved from: http://www.huffingtonpost.com/2013/02/01/arnold-schwarzenegger-green-activism_n_2598639.html

226 Pomfret, J. (2006 Dec 23). Schwarzenegger Remakes Himself as Environmentalist. *Washington Post.* Retrieved from: http://www.washingtonpost.com/wp-dyn/content/article/2006/12/22/AR2006122201476.html

227 Christopher T. Giovinazzo, California's Global Warming Bill: Will Fuel Economy Preemption Curb California's Air Pollution Leadership, 30 Ecology L.Q. (2003). Available at: http://scholarship.law.berkeley.edu/elq/vol30/iss4/2

228 California Air Resources Board. (2013 May 6). Clean Car Standards – Pavley, Assembly Bill 1493. Retrieved from: http://www.arb.ca.gov/cc/ccms/ccms.htm

229 U.S. Department of Transportation. (2014 Aug 27). Corporate Average Fuel Economy (CAFE) Standards. Retrieved from:

https://www.transportation.gov/mission/sustainability/corporate-average-fuel-economy-cafe-standards

230 Ibid.
231 Kuchta, R. (2002 Jul 24). Gov. Davis signs precedent-setting vehicle emission bill. *Malibu Times.* Retrieved from: http://www.malibutimes.com/news/article_5e1300e5-efcf-59f0-9eef-7196a1d4661c.html
232 Ibid.
233 Ibid.
234 Claybrook, J (2008 Feb 29) EPA Denies California Global Warning Emission Standards for Cars. Public Citizen.
235 Hakim, D. (2006 Apr 28). 10 States Sue EPA on Emissions. *New York Times.* Retrieved from: http://www.nytimes.com/2006/04/28/us/28emissions.html?_r=0
236 Nat'l Research Council Comm. on State Practices in Setting Mobile Source Emissions Standards,. (2006). State and Federal Standards for Mobile-Source Emissions.
237 Beveridge & Diamond, P.C. (2007 Dec 13). Federal Judge Upholds California Law Regulating Greenhouse Gas Emissions from Motor Vehicles. Retrieved from: http://www.bdlaw.com/news-256.html
238 Freeman, S. (2007 Sept 13). Carmakers Defeated on Emission Rules. *Washington Post.* Retrieved from: http://www.washingtonpost.com/wp-dyn/content/article/2007/09/12/AR2007091202391.html
239 Wilson, J. & Reiterman, T. (2007 Apr 3). Greenhouse-gas law could still face hurdles. *Los Angeles Times.* Retrieved from: http://articles.latimes.com/2007/apr/03/local/me-greencalif3
240 McCarthy, J. & Meltz, R. (2008 Jan 8). California's Waiver Request to Control Greenhouse Gases under the Clean Air Act. CRS Report for Congress.
241 Davies, F. (2008 Feb 27). Internal Memos Show Pressure on EPA Chief. *East Bay Times.* Retrieved from: http://www.eastbaytimes.com/oaklandtribune/localnews/ci_8377071
242 Maynard, M., (2007 Dec. 19). EPA Denies California Emissions Waiver. *New York Times.* Retrieved from: http://www.nytimes.com/2007/12/19/washington/20epa-web.html?_r=0

243 Lifsher, M. (2007 Nov 9). Gov. sues U.S. over clean-air standards. *Los Angeles Times*. Retrieved from: http://articles.latimes. com/2007/nov/09/business/fi-warm9

244 Crawley, J. (2008 Mar 1). California emission waiver formally blocked. Reuters. Retrieved from: http://www.reuters.com/article/ environment-climate-california-dc-idUSN2922095420080301

245 Bensinger, K. & Tankersley, J. (2009 Jan 26). Obama to give California emission rules another look. *Los Angeles Times*. Retrieved from: http://articles.latimes.com/2009/jan/26/nation/ na-emissions26

246 Tankersley, J. (2009 Jun 30). EPA gives California emissions waiver. *Los Angeles Times*. Retrieved from http://articles.lat-imes.com/2009/jun/30/nation/na-california-waiver30

247 Public Policy Institute of California (2016 July). PPIC Statewide Survey: Californians and the Environment. Retrieved from: http://www.ppic.org/main/pressrelease.asp?p=2055

248 California Air Resources Board. Climate Change Draft Scoping Plan: Economic Analysis Supplement. State of California. Retrieved from: http://www.arb.ca.gov/cc/scopingplan/docu-ment/economic_analysis_supplement.pdf

249 Go Solar California. Net Energy Metering in California. Retrieved from: http://www.gosolarcalifornia.ca.gov/solar_basics/net_me-tering.php

250 Ibid.

251 California Public Utilities Commission. Net Energy Metering (NEM). Retrieved from: http://www.cpuc.ca.gov/General.aspx? id=3800

252 Ibid.

253 California Climate & Agriculture Network. (2015 Jun). Net Metering: Improving On-Farm Clean Energy Rules. Retrieved from: http://calclimateag.org/net-metering/

254 Ibid.

255 Hsu, T. (2009 Oct 13). Schwarzenegger signs 2 renewable en-ergy bills, vetoes others. *Los Angeles Times*. Retrieved from: http://articles.latimes.com/2009/oct/13/business/fi-solar13

256 California Public Utilities Commission. Virtual Net Metering. Retrieved from: http://www.cpuc.ca.gov/General.aspx?id= 5408

257 Energy & Policy Institute. California Net Metering Attacks. Retrieved from: http://www.energyandpolicy.org/california-net-metering-attacks

258 Ibid.

259 Lacey, S. (2014 Nov 4). The End of a Solar Era: The Legacy of the California Solar Initiative. Greentech Media. Retrieved from: http://www.greentechmedia.com/articles/read/the-legacy-of-the-california-solar-initiative

260 California Energy Commission. Actual and Expected Energy From Coal for California Overview. Retrieved from: http://www.energy.ca.gov/renewables/tracking_progress/documents/current_expected_energy_from_coal.pdf

261 Institute for Energy Research. (2015 Oct 22). California's Hidden Coal Use. Retrieved from: http://instituteforenergyresearch.org/analysis/californias-hidden-coal-use/

262 California Energy Commission. Actual and Expected Energy From Coal for California Overview. Retrieved from: http://www.energy.ca.gov/renewables/tracking_progress/documents/current_expected_energy_from_coal.pdf

263 Institute for Energy Research. (2015 Oct 22). California's Hidden Coal Use. Retrieved from: http://instituteforenergyresearch.org/analysis/californias-hidden-coal-use/

264 The Center for Land Use Interpretation. (2014). LADWP Power. Retrieved from: http://www.clui.org/newsletter/winter-2014/ladwp-power

265 Ibid.

266 Southern California Edison. 2005 Annual Report. Retrieved from: https://www.edison.com/content/dam/eix/documents/investors/sec-filings-financials/c6591_2005_SCE_annual_7189.pdf

267 Southern California Edison. (2013 Dec 30). Filing Letter – Four Corners Final.

268 Linthicum, K. (2013 Apr 23). L.A. City Council votes to move away from coal-fired energy. Los Angeles Times. Retrieved from: http://articles.latimes.com/2013/apr/23/local/la-me-ln-council-coal-energy-20130423

269 NRDC. (2006 Sept 29). Governor Signs Bill to Limit Dirty Power Generation. Retrieved from: https://www.nrdc.org/media/2006/060929-0

270 Ibid.
271 Douglass, E. (2008 Apr. 29). "Climate Think Tank's Legality Questioned," *Los Angeles Times*. Retrieved from http://articles. latimes.com/2008/apr/29/business/fi-institute29
272 Howard, J (2008 June 5). "PUC Institute at UC Kindles Suspicions," *Capitol Weekly*. Retrieved from: http://capitolweekly.net/puc-approved-institute-at-uc-kindles-suspicions/
273
274 York, A. & Howard, J. (2008 Aug 14). Greenhouse gas institute slips under the radar. *Capitol Weekly*.
275 Ibid.
276 Howard, J. (2008 Oct 2). Governor rejects climate-change institute at UC. *Capital Weekly*. Retrieved from: http://capitolweekly.net/governor-rejects-climate-change-institute-at-uc/
277 Watson, J. (2015 Oct 27). University of California unveils plan to curb climate change. Associated Press.
278 San Diego Gas & Electric. (2007 Apr 12). SDG&E's "smart meter" program receives final state approval. Retrieved from: http://www.sdge.com/es/node/1727
279 Ibid.
280 California Public Utilities Commission. (2008 Sept 18). Decision Approving Settlement on Southern California Edison Company Advanced Metering Infrastructure Deployment. Retrieved from: http://docs.cpuc.ca.gov/PUBLISHED/FINAL_DECISION/91154.htm
281 California Public Utilities Commission. (2008 Apr 8). Decision on Application of Southern California Gas Company for Approval of Advanced Metering Infrastructure: Summary of Application. Retrieved from: http://docs.cpuc.ca.gov/PUBLISHED/FINAL_DECISION/116294-04.htm#P104_13052
282 California Public Utilities Commission. The Benefits of Smart Meters. Retrieved from: http://www.cpuc.ca.gov/General.aspx?id=4853&cmsMode=Preview
283 California Public Utilities Commission. (2012 Feb 1). PUC Approves Analog Meters for PG&E Customers Electing to Opt-Out of Smart Meter Service. Retrieved from: http://docs.cpuc.ca.gov/PUBLISHED/NEWS_RELEASE/158621.htm

284 Wilson Sonsini Goodrich & Rosati. (2016 Feb 1). WSGR Alert: California Public Utility Commission Approves Successor Net Energy Metering Tariff. Retrieved from: https://www.wsgr.com/ WSGR/Display.aspx?SectionName=publications/PDFSearch/ wsgralert-net-metering.htm

285 Natural Resources Defense Council. (2005 Sept 22). California Launches Biggest Energy Efficiency Program in History. Retrieved from: https://www.nrdc.org/media/2005/050922

286 Ballotpedia. "California Gubernatorial Election, 2010." Retrieved from: https://ballotpedia.org/California_gubernatorial_election,_2010

287 Roosevelt, M. (2010 Jun 23). Bid to suspend California's global warming law qualifies for November Ballot. *Los Angeles Times*. Retrieved from: http://articles.latimes.com/2010/jun/23/local/la-me-climate-initiative-20100623

288 Roosevelt, M. (2010 Jun 23). Bid to suspend California's global warming law qualifies for November Ballot. *Los Angeles Times*. Retrieved from: http://articles.latimes.com/2010/jun/23/local/la-me-climate-initiative-20100623

289 Public Policy Institute of California (2010 July 28) PPIC Statewide Survey: Californians and the Environment. Retrieved from: http://www.ppic.org/content/pubs/survey/S_710MBS.pdf

290 Roosevelt, M. (2010 Jul 28). Global warming: battle over California ballot initiative heats up. *Los Angeles Times*. Retrieved from: http://latimesblogs.latimes.com/greenspace/2010/07/global-warming-prop-23-california.html

291 Roosevelt, M. (2010 Jul 28). Global warming: battle over California ballot initiative heats up. *Los Angeles Times*. Retrieved from: http://latimesblogs.latimes.com/greenspace/2010/07/global-warming-prop-23-california.html

292 Rogers, P. (2010 May 3). Opponents of California Global Warming Law Turn in Signatures for November Measure. *Mercury News*.

293 Vara, V. (2010 Sept 17). Refiners Fight Emission Law. *Wall Street Journal*. Retrieved from: http://www.wsj.com/articles/SB10001424052748704394704575495902377602556

294 Roosevelt,M (2010 Nov 2). Proposition 23: Backers Were Outspent, Out-organized. Retrieved from: http://latimesblogs.latimes.com/greenspace/2010/11/proposition-23-defeat-global-warming-climate-change-initiative.html

295 Sullivan, C. & Kahn, D. (2010 Nov 3). Voters Reject 2-Sided Assault on Climate Law. *New York Times*. Retrieved from: http://www.nytimes.com/cwire/2010/11/03/03climatewire-voters-reject-2-sided-assault-on-climate-law-13439.html?pagewanted=all

296 Ibid.

297 Boxall, B. & York, A. (2012 Jul 26). Gov. Brown pushes $23-billion plan to tunnel under delta. *Los Angeles Times*. Retrieved from: http://articles.latimes.com/2012/jul/26/local/la-me-water-tunnel-20120726

298 LeBeau, P. (2015 July 29). Americans Holding on to Their Cars Longer Than Ever. CNBC. Retrieved from: http://www.cnbc.com/2015/07/28/americans-holding-onto-their-cars-longer-than-ever.html

299 Ayre, J. (2017 January 20). California Has ~50% of US Electric Cars. Retrieved from: http://www.ev-volumes.com/news/usa-plug-in-vehicle-sales-for-2016/

300 Kordus, D. (2017 January). Californians' Views on Climate Change. Public Policy Institute of California. Retrieved from: http://www.ppic.org/main/publication_show.asp?i=1172

Index